I0199919

Courage to Bear Witness

Books by Gene L. Davenport

What's the Church For?
The Eschatology of the Book of Jubilees
King Jesus: Servant, Lord, Soul Brother
Into the Darkness: Discipleship According to the Sermon on the Mount
Powers and Principalities
Though the Mountains Shake

Courage to Bear Witness

Essays in Honor of Gene L. Davenport

L. EDWARD PHILLIPS
& BILLY VAUGHAN, editors

☙PICKWICK *Publications* · Eugene, Oregon

COURAGE TO BEAR WITNESS
Essays in Honor of Gene L. Davenport

Copyright © 2009 Wipf and Stock Publishers. All rights reserved. Except for brief quotations in critical publications or reviews, no part of this book may be reproduced in any manner without prior written permission from the publisher. Write: Permissions, Wipf and Stock Publishers, 199 W. 8th Ave., Suite 3, Eugene, OR 97401.

Pickwick Publications
A Division of Wipf and Stock Publishers
199 W. 8th Ave., Suite 3
Eugene, OR 97401

www.wipfandstock.com

ISBN 13: 9781498253239

Cataloging-in-Publication data:

Courage to bear witness : essays in honor of Gene L. Davenport / edited by L. Edward Phillips and Billy Vaughan.

xii + 158 p. ; 23 cm.

ISBN 13: 9781498253239

1. Davenport, Gene L. 2. Davenport, Gene L.—Bibliography. 3. Methodism—history. 4. I. Phillips, L. Edward. II. Vaughan, Billy. III. Title.

BR50 2009

To Gene L. Davenport,
courageous witness

That night the Lord stood near him and said, "Keep up your courage!
For just as you have testified for me in Jerusalem, so you must bear
witness also in Rome."
Acts 23:11

Contents

Contributors

Kenneth L. Carder is the Ruth W. and A. Morris Williams Professor of the Practice of Christian Ministry at the Divinity School of Duke University in Durham, North Carolina, and a bishop (retired) of the United Methodist Church.

Randy Cooper is the Pastor of First United Methodist Church in Ripley, Tennessee, and Chair of the Order of Elders for the Memphis Annual Conference.

Stanley Hauerwas is the Gilbert T. Rowe Professor of Theological Ethics at Divinity School of Duke University in Durham, North Carolina.

James T. Laney is the President Emeritus of Emory University in Atlanta, Georgia, and the former Ambassador of the United States to South Korea.

D. Brent Laytham is the Professor of Theology and Ethics at North Park Theological Seminary in Chicago, Illinois, and Coordinator of The Ekklesia Project.

Charles Mayo is Professor of English, Chair of the Department of English, and Head of the School of Humanities at Lambuth University in Jackson, Tennessee.

M. Douglas Meeks is the Cal Turner Chancellor Professor of Theology and Wesleyan Studies at Vanderbilt University Divinity School in Nashville, Tennessee.

Margaret J. Meyer served as rabbi of Congregation B'nai Israel in Jackson, Tennessee, from 1999–2008. She lives in Cincinnati, Ohio, where she teaches Hebrew and Jewish studies.

L. Edward Phillips is Associate Professor of Worship and Liturgical Theology at the Candler School of Theology of Emory University in Atlanta, Georgia.

Joseph T. Reiff is Associate Professor of Religion and Chair of the Department of Religion at Emory & Henry College in Emory, Virginia.

Tex Sample is the Robert B. and Kathleen Rogers Professor Emeritus of Church and Society at Saint Paul School of Theology in Kansas City, Missouri.

Phyllis Tickle is a Senior Fellow of Cathedral College of the Washington National Cathedral and former editor of the Religion Department of *Publishers Weekly*.

Billy Vaughan is co-director of The Memphis School of Servant Leadership and works with the Sustaining Pastoral Excellence and Formation For Ministry programs at Memphis Theological Seminary in Memphis, Tennessee.

Cindy Wesley is Associate Professor of Religion and Chair of the Department of Religion and Philosophy at Lambuth University in Jackson, Tennessee.

Foreword

It has long been customary to present a collection of essays to honor the accomplishments of an esteemed colleague in the academy on the occasion of his or her retirement. The German word for such a collection, *Festschrift*, literally means "festival writing." It is a joyous task, one that acknowledges a debt of gratitude for the life and work of the individual so honored. In this volume, we acknowledge our debt of gratitude to Gene L. Davenport, whose courageous and intellectually rigorous witness to the Gospel has inspired and challenged many lives throughout his long tenure as Professor of Religion at Lambuth University in Jackson, Tennessee, and as a minister in the United Methodist Church.

More often than not, history is told as the story of presidents, generals, popes, bishops, famous intellectuals, and persons with extraordinary wealth: told as major events on a world stage. Most of history, however, takes place in our local communities, and this has been the venue of Gene Davenport. In his ministry in West Tennessee, Gene has worked courageously in the trenches, addressing racism, the demon of American nationalism, and the hope of ecumenical and inter-religious friendship. He is an academic with expertise in biblical and pseudepigraphic literature who has also served as pastor of small, rural United Methodist congregations. He is a professional singer of "Cowboy Music" who also knows the Hebrew of the ancient songs of Israel. He has published in the academic press, but also for the Sunday school press, and he has a regular column his local newspaper, *The Jackson Sun*. In all these endeavors, Gene embodies what he has taught his students: a Christian does not try to "change the world," but seeks to live a changed life as an obedient disciple of the one who has already fundamentally changed the world, though the world does not yet know this.

As editors of this volume, we are deeply grateful to the contributors for their fine work. We are certain that we speak for all the contributors in saying it has been an honor to celebrate the life and work of Gene by means of this *Festschrift*. Gene has been a teacher and mentor for some of us, a colleague in education and ministry for others, and a good and loyal friend to all. We represent a small number of Gene's friends who, we are sure, would have been glad to contribute had we only the foresight to ask. We especially acknowledge Will Campbell who gave us good advice (and who has a deep love for Gene), but who was unable to make a written contribution at this time.

Randy Cooper was part of the original meeting where the idea for this *Festschrift* was born, and he has continued to advise us along the way. Our wives, Sara Webb Phillips and Joni Laney, have read and made helpful comments on these essays. Jacob Chambliss, Ed's student assistant, checked footnotes and also helped with the editing. Roy Herron and Nancy Miller Herron offered financial support for this project. All of these have helped bring this book to completion, and we thank all of them for their contributions.

It was Stanley Hauerwas who suggested we contact Charlie Collier at Wipf and Stock Publishers. It is becoming rare for publishers to accept a proposal for a *Festschrift*, and we are grateful that Wipf and Stock has published this labor of love.

Stephen's Storied Witness to Jesus

D. Brent Laytham

I first encountered Gene Davenport in the pages of his *Into the Darkness*. There Will Campbell's "Foreword" retold Gene's courageous confronta-tion with the KKK while a young pastor in Mississippi.[1] That story, well placed to introduce Gene's *Into the Darkness*, is also a proper introduc-tion to Gene himself, a man for whom courage is second nature, and witness a way of life.

Though separated by two millennia, I find considerable common ground between this story and that of the church's first martyr Stephen (Acts 6–7). Both stories involve a sudden confrontation (Acts 6:12) be-tween a lone preacher and a hostile, culturally powerful group intent on sustaining its customs and institutions (see 6:14). Moreover, both inci-dents center on proper worship, since both the accosting group and the accosted preacher worship the same God (at least ostensibly they do) and belong to the same community of faith. Both stories are fraught with the threat of deadly violence, and both center in dispute about the pattern of God's will as revealed in the scriptural story. In each story the preacher bears courageous witness, both in word and deed, that the Righteous One has now opened heaven to all God's children, no matter who or where they are. And in both stories, what the courageous witness actually says "is clearly not intended to soothe its audience."[2]

Now of course, there are also clear differences: to my knowledge no one claimed on that night in Mississippi that Gene's "face was like the

---

1. Will Campbell, "Foreword," in Gene Davenport, *Into the Darkness: Discipleship in the Sermon on the Mount* (Nashville: Abingdon, 1988) 9–11.

2. This is Robert Tannehill's description of Stephen's speech in *The Narrative Unity of Luke–Acts: A Literary Interpretation*, 2 vols. (Philadelphia: Fortress, 1986) 2:85. It is equally apt for Campbell's description of Davenport's actions that night.

1

face of an angel" (Acts 6:15). But there is enough common ground that a look at Stephen's story will properly honor Gene precisely by focusing our attention on the church's calling to bear faithful witness (Acts 1:8) to Jesus Christ, "the faithful and true witness" (Rev 3:14).

Much of this essay focuses on Stephen's "speech" (Acts 7:2–53)[3] in order to display how his narrative rendering of Scripture already is a witness to Christ, and how it funds his witness unto death.[4] A key objection surfaces immediately, however; the exegetical claim that Stephen's speech has very little to say about Jesus. This objection can be restated as the question of whether Stephen is properly labeled a witness. Despite the fact that later in Acts Paul clearly calls Stephen a witness (22:20), one could argue that Stephen fails to meet the minimal criterion—inasmuch as Jesus commissioned his followers to be "*my* witnesses" (1:8).[5] For in this longest speech in Acts, Stephen does not have much to say (explicitly) about Jesus.[6] Heretofore in Acts, Jesus has been the obvious center and subject matter of all four of Peter's speeches, as he will be for most

3. I will not engage the extensive discussion of the precise genre of this material, nor questions about whether it represents a theological perspective that differs from Luke's. My concern is the scriptural Stephen that Luke has rendered for us here. I find questions about the historical Stephen theologically uninteresting.

4. Here I work in the vein of the nine theses of "The Scripture Project." Specifically, I believe that Acts 7 provides evidence for the claim that Scripture is best understood "as a coherent dramatic narrative," and that to faithfully interpret Scripture "requires an engagement with the entire narrative" of the Bible. Ellen F. Davis and Richard B. Hays, eds., *The Art of Reading Scripture* (Grand Rapids: Eerdmans, 2003) 1–5, quotations from pages 1 and 2 respectively.

5. Given the emphasis in Acts on a witness (*martyr*) as one who has *seen* "everything [Jesus] did in the country of the Jews and in Jerusalem" (10:39; see also 1:21–22) and has also *seen* Jesus risen from the dead (10:41; see also 2:32; 3:15; 5:32; 13:31), Stephen wouldn't qualify. Stephen is not represented as one who walked with Jesus in his ministry, nor as one who had seen the risen Christ—at least not until the culmination of his story (7:56). Marion Soards has an excellent discussion of the expansion of the category of witness as Luke moves from his gospel to Acts. "As the story continues in Acts, those referred to as witnesses and those overtly bearing witness prove to be more than the Twelve." *The Speeches in Acts: Their Content, Context, and Concerns* (Louisville: Westminster John Knox, 1994) 197. Soards lists five groups/persons who are called witnesses: 1) apostles, 2) the Holy Spirit, 3) Paul, 4) Stephen, and 5) the false witnesses.

6. "It seems clear that Stephen's speech . . . lacks that witness to Jesus which characterizes the usual Acts speech." John J. Killagen, S.J., "The Function of Stephen's Speech (Acts 7:2–53)," *Biblica* 70 (1989) 173–93; 182. Later Killagen adds ". . . Jesus only comes to the fore in the last sentence of the speech. Even here, Jesus is not named, but is rather a further example . . ." (183).

of Paul's speeches hereafter. This leads Marion Soards to conclude that Stephen's speech displays a "lack of standard kerygma."[7] Other scholars say that Stephen was finally killed not because he was witnessing *to* Jesus, but because he was speaking *against* the Temple.[8] So given that the bulk of Stephen's speech is a retelling of Israel's story, can we properly claim that he is a witness *to Jesus*? I hope to show in what follows that we can.

Our consideration of the story Stephen tells must begin with the provocative claim of James Alison, who notes:

> [Stephen's] defense consists in *an attempt to tell the story of Israel anew*, a revisionist rewriting. . . . What Stephen does is to tell the story which everybody already knew, from rather an odd angle, from the angle which came to light after the Holy Spirit made it possible to tell the story of the lynch from the viewpoint of the victim.[9]

One does not have to adopt Alison's Girardian lens to recognize that he is correct to highlight the different angle of vision opened by Jesus' crucifixion–resurrection–ascension. To put that point differently, Stephen's speech is not primarily his defense against the allegation that he has attacked the temple and the Torah, but is rather his witness to Jesus by retelling the scriptural story *from the point of view of Jesus at God's right hand.*

Telling the story from that point of view leaves God as the central character. The first agent and the prime subject of this story is not Israel, but "the God of glory" (7:2). In the first six verses of the speech, "God is the subject of every main verb" except one, and "without these verbs the story has no movement . . ."[10] Moreover, Stephen makes narratological choices which highlight divine (rather than human) agency. For example, Stephen places Abraham's call all the way back in Mesopotamia "before

---

7. Soards, *Speeches*, 69.

8. See the discussion in James P. Sweeney, "Stephen's Speech (Acts 7:2–53): Is It as 'Anti-Temple' as Is Frequently Alleged?" *Trinity Journal* (2002) 185–210; 187.

9. James Alison, *Raising Abel: The Recovery of the Eschatological Imagination* (New York: Crossroad, 1996) 79 (emphasis mine).

10. John Kilgallen, *The Stephen Speech* (Rome: Biblical Institute Press, 1976) 43. For a discussion of the nuanced ways Acts 7 centers on God, see Soards, *Speeches*, 61–65. In this regard, Stephen's speech shares a similar structure with Peter's Pentecost sermon, which at its core reiterates three times that God has acted by raising (or exalting) Jesus (2:24, 32, 36; see further claims of divine agency at 2:17–18, 22, 23, 33, 34).

he lived in Haran" (Acts 7:2), even though the Genesis travelogue seems to place that call in Haran after Terah's death (see Gen 11:31—12:5).[11] This apparent replotting is not a mistake on Stephen's part, or an example of "storyteller's license." Rather, it is Stephen giving narrative priority to God's self-identification in Gen 15:7, where God says "I am the Lord who brought you out from Ur of the Chaldeans . . ."; Stephen notices that God did not say "who brought you out of Haran," and so he tells the story accordingly.

In telling the story this way, three emphases emerge. First, Stephen emphasizes God's *prevenience* in Abraham's story; everything depends on God's prior, initiatory activity. Abraham did not decide to go looking for God by moving westward; instead, he was found, claimed, and called out of Ur by God. Second, this emphasizes that God found Abraham "outside the land," a motif that Stephen also works into his characterization of the stories of Joseph and Moses.[12] Thus God's presence and providence are not geographically bounded; indeed, Stephen tells the story as one where God's greatest provision regularly occurs outside the land of promise. Finally, Stephen's telling suggests that God refuses to be God in solitary glory, electing rather to claim and call forth Israel as the community that exists to worship God in holiness and justice (see Zechariah's hymn at Luke 1:68–79).[13]

That God is preveniently active was not news to Stephen's hearers. What was news—indeed good news, though they did not hear it as such—was Stephen's identification of Jesus with the God whose story he tells. Stephen does this most fully when he addresses Jesus in prayer as "Lord" (for more on this, see below). In this regard James Alison is exactly right to argue that Stephen's "Look, I see the heavens opened" is not so much a sudden vision given to Stephen at the moment of his dying, as it is an ongoing way of seeing the world and its story.[14] In other words,

11. See Kilgallen, *Stephen Speech*, 42, for analysis of this.

12. For analysis of the "God outside the land" motif, see Rex Koivisto, "Stephen's Speech: A Theology of Errors?" *Grace Theological Journal* 8 (1987) 101–14.

13. Kilgallen says that "the statement of God to Abraham is nothing short of a correct justification for the existence of Israel. Israel is created 'to worship Me in this place.'" John J. Kilgallen, S.J., "The Speech of Stephen, Acts 7:2-53," *The Expository Times* 115 (2004) 293–97; 293. Koivisto believes that the reference to Terah's death at 7:4 also exemplifies Stephen's concern with "pure devotion to Yahweh" (111–13). On this relation to Zechariah's doxology, see Kilgallen, "Speech of Stephen," 293n14.

14. Alison, *Raising Abel*, 79–80.

because Stephen already sees "the heavens opened" (7:56), because he already sees Jesus in the midst of God's glory (7:55), because he recognizes that Jesus is the culmination of God's agency and the revelation of God's identity, he can offer a radical retelling of Israel's story.

Thus, Stephen's retelling is a powerful example of how the end of this story finally determines its real shape and true meaning. David Steinmetz claims that "the church's traditional exegesis" knew well that "how the story ends makes a difference for the beginning and middle of the story as well as for its conclusion."[15] I would suggest that the church's exegetes learned this reading strategy from our Gospel writers, who found it necessary "to read earlier parts of the Bible in the light of later developments."[16] Indeed, this is precisely what we find in Acts 7: Stephen offers "what amounts to a radically different interpretation of the OT" because of his "conviction that the whole story of God's redemptive work had reached its fulfillment in the coming of that Righteous One (Acts 7:52). . . ."[17] Stephen's retelling of Israel's story in light of Christ's ascension is "the disclosure of the architectonic structure of the whole story"; it is "a compelling and persuasive disclosure of what the story was about all along."[18] That is to say, even without mentioning Jesus' name, Stephen rehearses Scripture as a story plotted toward Jesus. Thereby Stephen bears witness to Jesus, and shows us that our own work of witness requires a proper grounding in a particular, narrative way of reading Scripture from the point of view of the end revealed in Jesus Christ.[19]

Another indication of how Stephen tells God's story from the perspective of the end revealed in Jesus Christ is that he crafts an overall narrative arc that tells the story from Israel's beginning until his hearer's

15. David Steinmetz, "Uncovering a Second Narrative: Detective Fiction and the Construction of Historical Method," in Hays and Davis, *Art of Reading Scripture*, 54.

16. Ibid. Though this is Steinmetz's characterization of the pre-modern exegetical tradition, I think it first describes the exegetical strategy of the authors of the NT.

17. Martin H. Sharlemann, *Stephen: A Singular Saint* (Rome: Pontifical Biblical Institute, 1968) 57.

18. This is Steinmetz's characterization (55) of the inevitable retelling of the story at the end of a detective novel. He uses this comparison to explain and justify narrative readings of Scripture, rather than to comment specifically on Acts 7 (which is only mentioned at 56n1).

19. For a more extensive discussion of the way the story is shaped by its ending in Christ, see my reading of Acts 2, "The Narrative Shape of Scriptural Authority: Plotting Pentecost," *Ex Auditu* 19 (2003) 97–119.

"now," a present moment defined by the fate of Jesus.[20] This is signaled near the beginning of the story, when Stephen refers to God's leading Abraham "to this country in which you are *now* living" (7:4). The culmination of the story, however, is not settlement of the land (7:45), but the present moment of the speech—a moment determined by the fate of Jesus. Stephen's narration culminates with the claim "and *now* you have become [Jesus'] betrayers and murderers" (7:52), thereby incorporating his hearers within the story in terms of Jesus crucified and risen.[21]

Closely related to the way temporal signals are used to include the hearers in the story is the function of pronouns. Stephen uses first person plural pronouns to invoke community with his hearers at the beginning of his retelling by reference to "*our* ancestor Abraham" (7:2; see also "our ancestors" at 11–12, 15, 19, 38–39, 44–45; "our people" at 17; "our race" at 19; and "us" at 38). Describing the revelation at Sinai, Stephen says that Moses "received living oracles to give *to us*" (38) rather than saying "to them"—indicating that Israel remains one people through time. Yet for all the work these pronouns do to place Stephen and his hearers within the same community, there remains a fundamental difference between him and them. That difference is revealed in both instances of the "narrative now," because Stephen says "you" rather than "we." At 7:4b he says "this country in which *you* are now living,"[22] a foreshadowing of the six rapid and emphatic uses of "you" and "yours" at the end of the speech in his hearer's present reality (7:51–53).

It might appear that Stephen has laid a rhetorical trap by speaking a pronominal community into existence only to renounce it polemically. In fact, this is Stephen's storied acknowledgement that God's single people, having received God's law and God's Righteous One, has not responded singularly. Rather, some have opposed what others have welcomed—God's working by Word and Spirit. Of course, his focus in this telling is on the history of opposition. He recounts how "our forefathers" jealously

20. For the senses of "now" in Acts, see Soards, *Speeches*, 190–91.

21. Soards has argued that this is a common feature of the speeches in Acts: Israel's past and the church's present and future are all determined by how the story ends in Christ. "Thus, Israel's past is recalled in Acts as it is related to Jesus Christ, and the church's present and future both have their meaning in relation to God's work in Jesus Christ, which determines the character and course of every new moment." Soards, *Speeches*, 189.

22. According to Soards, "The statement creates distance between Stephen and the audience he is addressing and is the first hint of the polemical character of the address." *Speeches*, 62.

tried to kill Joseph, repeatedly turned against Moses, and persecuted the prophets, establishing an ongoing pattern that finds its culmination in the crucifixion of Jesus and its continuation in the present persecution of Stephen.[23] So now Stephen, ostensibly the accused, tells God's story in a way that does accuse the Sanhedrin.

But that does not make this story non-kerygmatic, a far cry from the way earlier speeches concluded with calls for repentance and/or proclamations of salvation (e.g. 2:38; 3:26; 4:12; 5:31). Recognizing that "this is the language of prophetic indictment, and its key terms are drawn from the Scriptures,"[24] we can see that, even where unspoken, there is an implicit call for repentance. Stephen's accusation of the Sanhedrin is necessary to the possibility of their genuine repentance, for accepting God's forgiveness always entails assent that we are indeed guilty of that for which we are being forgiven.[25] Far from picking a fight here, Stephen is actually narrating the need for the forgiveness that he will shortly petition Jesus to offer (7:60).

Because Stephen tells God's story plotted toward Jesus, his speech is bearing witness even when Jesus is not explicitly named. We see that even more clearly by attending to key typological relations in his telling. First is Joseph, who was rejected and afflicted by jealous brethren, "but God was with him" (7:9). The shape of Stephen's retelling of the Joseph story, according to John Kilgallen, is this: "the one who saves is the one who has been rejected, he saves those who rejected him, and he saved them precisely through their having rejected him. . . ."[26] Attention to Stephen's narrative vocabulary at this point strengthens the typological relationship, not only with Jesus, but also with faithful disciples like Stephen. Kilgallen points to the attribution of wisdom (*sophia*) to Joseph (7:10), a term that seems warranted by the story in Genesis 37–50 even though it is not present there. It is, however, an important word in Luke-Acts. In Luke

---

23. Thus there is continuity between fathers and sons: ". . . *they* killed the ones who prophesied the coming of the one *you* have killed; in this way the children not only act like their fathers, but bring their fathers' evil deeds to conclusion. . . . It is this completion of past in present that Stephen's speech wants to underline." Kilgallen, "Function," 175n5.

24. Sweeney, "Stephen's Speech," 208.

25. On this, see the clear work of Miroslav Volf, *Free of Charge* (Grand Rapids: Zondervan, 2005) 129ff. Volf says forcefully that "A condemnation of the wrongdoing is one element of forgiveness, its indispensable negative presupposition" (130).

26. Kilgallen, "Function," 186.

"wisdom" describes Jesus' maturation (2:40, 52), as well as something his disciples can hope for when *witnessing* in the face of persecution of the very sort Stephen now confronts (Luke 21:15 and see the full context vv. 12–19). In Acts 'wisdom' is one qualification of the seven deacons (Acts 6:3), a quality powerfully revealed in Stephen's public speaking (6:10 phrased as a direct fulfillment of the promise given at Luke 21:15).[27] So Stephen's brief overview of the Joseph portion of God's story is told with terminology that emphasizes a typological connection between Joseph, Jesus *and Stephen*. One crucial parallel between these three, beyond the mere fact of rejection and persecution by their own people, is the shape of their response to it: in each case, they forgive. Even though Stephen does not foreground this similarity in his recounting of the Joseph saga, it comes into play when Stephen intercedes for the forgiveness of his hearers.

The central typology is between Moses and Jesus, each one a rejected redeemer who was vindicated by God.[28] Stephen grounds this typological relation by referencing the Deuteronomy 18:15 claim that one day God will raise up a prophet like Moses (Acts 7:37). Though Stephen does not explicitly state that Jesus is the "prophet like Moses," this implicit point would not be lost on his hearers or readers. Indeed, readers know that Luke has already identified Jesus as a prophet "mighty in deed and word" in the Emmaus story (Luke 24:19)[29] and that Peter has referenced this prophecy in an earlier speech (Acts 3:22). Just as with Joseph, again with Moses there is a pattern of God's chosen one being rejected by God's people, yet still accomplishing God's purposed salvation; indeed, in Moses' case there is a double rejection, first in Egypt (7:25–29, 35) and then in the wilderness idolatry (7:39–41). F. F. Bruce finds a similar

27. Kilgallen, *Stephen's Speech*, 49–50. See also Kilgallen's claim that "affliction" (*thlipsis*) is a Lukan term placed on the Joseph narrative in a way that connects Joseph's experience with "those trials Christians undergo in their perseverance in faith" (*Stephen's Speech*, 50; see also his "Speech of Stephen," 294).

28. See H. Alan Brehm, "Vindicating the Rejected One: Stephen's Speech as a Critique of the Jewish Leaders," in Craig Evans and James Sanders, eds., *Early Christian Interpretation of the Scriptures of Israel: Investigations and Proposals* (Sheffield: Sheffield Academic Press, 1997) 266–99; 285; Soards, *Speeches*, 65; Tannehill, *Narrative Unity*, 2:91.

29. For more on the parallels between Acts 7 and Luke 24, see E. Jane Via, "An Interpretation of Acts 7:35–37 from the Perspective of Major Themes in Luke-Acts," *Perspectives in Religious Studies* 6 (1979) 190–207; see 205–6.

double rejection in that "Jesus, rejected during his earthly ministry, was rejected again when he was presented to the people as their leader and deliverer after his resurrection. The present generation was following the precedent of the wilderness generation."[30] In Moses' case, Kilgallen sees a further parallel with Jesus: he says that "without Moses, Israel lost its way. . . . Without the true mediator Israel lost contact with the true God. . . . The ancients gave up on Moses, and THEREFORE gave up on Yahweh and turned to a false idol for salvation."[31]

Stephen's rendering of Joseph and Moses as types of Christ suggests another typology implicit in his retelling of Israel's story: "your ancestors" are a type of "you stiff-necked people." Notice the logic at work in his earlier retelling: Joseph is a type of Christ not only because God was with Joseph, but also because his brothers were against him—even though Joseph (like Jesus) was God's chosen agent of rescue. And Moses is a type of Christ not only because God speaks and acts through him for Israel's rescue, but also because Israel repeatedly rejected this one sent by God (like Jesus) to be Israel's "ruler and liberator" (7:35). Thus, implicit in the descriptions of Joseph and Moses as types of Christ is the implication that those who refused them function typologically as precursor to the present generation which has refused Jesus. That typological connection is made explicit in Stephen's rhetorically powerful accusation that "just as your ancestors used to do," so you have done (7:51). In general, then, what we see is that these typologies find their place in Stephen's interpretation of the overall narrative arc of Scripture as the ongoing repetition of Yahweh's initiative and Israel's refusal, which always places Israel under judgment and often brings catastrophe, but which never finally defeats God's saving action.[32] Indeed, Israel's refusals are at times the very circumstance which God uses to save.[33]

Specifically, the rhetorical conclusion of Stephen's retelling brings together the way Stephen's audience has treated Jesus and is now treating Stephen. Note the charges that Stephen piles one after another. First, that

---

30. F. F. Bruce, "Stephen's Apologia," in Barry Thompson, ed., *Scripture: Meaning and Method* (Hull: Hull University Press, 1987) 37–50; 44.

31. Kilgallen, "Speech," 295 (capitalization original).

32. For discussion of this as a "Deuteronomic view of history," see Tannehill, *Narrative Unity*, 2:86–87, 94–95; Soards, *Speeches*, 94–97.

33. This is clearly the case with the rejection of Joseph, the crucifixion of Jesus, and (as Luke subsequently shows) with the stoning of Stephen.

Israel's history establishes typologically that, just as your ancestors did, so now "you are forever opposing the Holy Spirit" (7:51). Second, that just as "they killed those who foretold the coming of the Righteous One, [so] now you have become his betrayers and murderers" (7:52). In successive sentences, Stephen suggests that Israel's history is one continual story of resistance to the Spirit and the Son, with former generations functioning as a lesser type of the greater resistance of this present generation. This situates their response in an ongoing history of refusal without obscuring the qualitative difference involved in betraying and murdering Jesus.[34] Similarly, in relation to resisting the Holy Spirit there is both continuity and qualitative difference. Their resistance is not narrated as a direct refusal of Jesus (who after all is the unique bearer of the Holy Spirit in Luke), but as their ongoing resistance (in Acts) to Christ-ordained bearers of the Spirit like Stephen.[35] Here, ". . . Stephen is the bearer of the Spirit"[36]—not uniquely, of course, but in the sense promised by the ascending Christ (Acts 1:8). So their opposition to Stephen's message is not only another example in the ongoing history of resistance, but is also the culmination of that history in the qualitatively new situation in which God incarnate overwhelms all refusals.

Finally, we must note an overall pattern in Stephen's telling which Robert Tannehill calls "tragic reversal." The linguistic signal of this pattern is that Stephen uses "key terms first in a positive and then in a negative sense."[37] Whereas Abraham is resettled into the promised land (7:4), idolatrous Israel is resettled away from it (7:43). Similarly, God says that Abraham's descendants will "worship me in this place" (7:7), yet later in the wilderness Israel is "handed . . . over to worship the host of heaven" (7:42).[38] And the "covenant of circumcision" is first mentioned positively (7:8), while the second occurrence is profoundly accusatory (7:51). All three of these examples contribute to the overall shaping of Stephen's story

34. Kilgallen characterizes this difference as a bringing to "completion of past in present." "Function," 175n5.

35. "Opposition to his [Stephen's] message is but another example of the history of Jewish opposition to God's will (7:51–53)." Dennis D. Sylva, "The Meaning and Function of Acts 7:46-50," *Journal of Biblical Literature* 106 (1987) 261–75; 274.

36. For this quote, see Sylva, "Meaning and Function," 273, with supporting argument at 273–74.

37. Tannehill, *Narrative Unity*, 2:90.

38. See ibid.

as one which renders the present situation unsurprising in light of past history: God's redemptive agent has been rejected and killed, ostensibly in defense of covenant faithfulness and proper worship. Indeed proper worship is a crucial concern in this retelling of the story, which is claiming in its own subtle way that worshiping God is the goal of Abraham's call and the reason Israel exists.[39]

If most interpreters have focused primarily on how such a construal of the scriptural story challenges or accuses the accusers, I suggest we ask instead how it actually funds Stephen's capacity for embodied witness. In this regard, James Alison has properly called our attention to the way Stephen's vision of Christ ascended into an open heaven gives Stephen the capacity to witness that God's redemptive purpose has triumphed and that forgiveness continues to be offered. To put the matter differently, I think that interpreters who think the speech embodies a Deuteronomic view that historical catastrophes (like the Exile) are proper judgments of God attend too much to the question of the destruction of the Temple, and attend too little to the subsequent manner of Stephen's destruction. Yes, readers of Acts would certainly have been aware that the question of the Temple's destruction—by Jesus or anybody else—had become moot with the Roman destruction of it in 70 C.E. But I contend that neither Stephen's deployment of this pattern of tragic reversal nor his careful emphasis on God's availability beyond the bounds of the promised land, nor even his direct de-centering of the Temple (7:44–50) in favor of divine transcendence, is primarily intended to offer a subtle response to the charge that he "never stops saying things against this holy place" (6:13 and see 14). Rather, it is all oriented toward the glory of God, a terminological repetition that brackets the whole speech (7:2 and 55) in a different pattern than tragic reversal. The true pattern, deeper and wider than "the tired story of the violence of the world,"[40] is God's initiating, enduring, and culminating agency for redeemed life with God. Stephen is narrating a comedy; he tells the story as he does, not to justify himself against the charge that he has opposed the temple and the law, and not even finally to charge his accusers with vitiating the law and turning from the temple's God, but simply to bring into speech and then action the

---

39. Thus Kilgallen, "Function," 180 and see also note 14.

40. Alison, *Raising Abel*, 78.

scriptural story he now lives: the forgiving glory of God beheld in the crucified and ascended Lord Jesus.

Because Stephen's auditors actively refused his rendition of the scriptural story as leading to a murdered, yet still forgiving, messiah, his speech concludes in martyrdom. Specifically, they cover their ears when Stephen includes Jesus in God's glory (and thus, in God's very identity), stoning him as a blasphemer. Which of course he is—if it is not true that Jesus is now "at the right hand of God" (7:55). Just as his Lord had read Moses and the prophets as leading to his risen flesh (Luke 24),[41] so Stephen also reads the scriptures. Just as his Lord died committing his spirit to God and petitioning for the forgiveness of his killers, so Stephen commits and petitions God—now identified as this very "Lord Jesus" who died and was raised.

Thus, Stephen began a pattern of the non-identical repetition of the dying of our Lord in which those who bear witness to Christ in their living perform the full measure of that witness in the cruciform pattern of their dying. Already in the late second century, martyrs and confessors drew on the story of Stephen for the shape of their own performative witness. So Eusebius reports that those being persecuted in Lyons "prayed for those who treated them so cruelly, as did Stephen, the fulfilled martyr: 'Lord, do not charge them with this sin.' If he pleaded for those who were stoning him, how much more for brother-Christians?"[42]

Such non-identical repetitions of a martyrdom like Stephen's were not limited to the early church. In *At the Hands of Persons Unknown: The Lynching of Black America*, Philip Dray tells the story of Edward Johnson, a black man wrongfully convicted of raping a white woman in Chattanooga, Tennessee. When Johnson's execution was stayed by appeal to the Supreme Court, a mob convened to hang him from the Walnut Street Bridge. When they demanded that he confess his guilt before dying, Johnson—a newly-baptized Christian—had this to say: "I am ready to die, but I never done it. . . . I am not guilty and that is all I have to

---

41. On this, see my "Interpretation on the Way to Emmaus: Jesus Performs His Story," *Journal of Theological Interpretation* 1 (2007) 101–15, esp. 102–8.

42. Eusebius, *The History of the Church from Christ to Constantine*, trans. G. A. Williamson (Baltimore: Penguin, 1965) 149. Eusebius also quotes Hegesippus' account of the martyrdom of James, in which James intercedes for those who stone him quoting Jesus' petition from the cross (Luke 23:34), *History* 60. There is clearly an established pattern of performing Christ's forgiving petition.

say. God bless you all. I am innocent."[43] Johnson was buried with these final two sentences engraved on his tombstone, a modern martyr to the same God-blessed story that Stephen told, to the same vision of a Christ-opened heaven that made Stephen, the martyrs in Lyons—and Gene Davenport, too—courageous witnesses.

43. Philip Dray, *At the Hands of Persons Unknown: The Lynching of Black America* (New York: Random House, 2002) 157, with the entire Johnson affair described at 152–59.

God's Gracious Judgment: A Theological Reflection

Randy Cooper

I learned a lot from Gene Davenport when I was a student and religion major at Lambuth College[1] in the early 1970s. Our sustained friendship has been ever since a means of grace for me. Indeed, I continue to learn from him.

I can still recall the first time I heard Gene preach to our Lambuth campus congregation. It was a Sunday morning in the spring of 1972. He wondered aloud if the church in the West is presently under the judgment of God. He was not himself casting judgment. He wore no mantle proclaiming that his was the voice of the Lord. He said what he said not because he liked saying it, but because Gene Davenport is not a supersessionist in regard to Scripture. That is, he believed then, and believes now, that the judgments pronounced on Israel by the prophetic Word of Scripture must also be heard as judgments upon the church. If the church bears through Christ the prophetic promises of Scripture, then through Christ the church also bears in its history the judgments of God.

This paper is little more than a response to that sermon in 1972. As a pastor, I live and work among the church's ruins.[2] I believe that the hand of the Lord's judgment is indeed raised. Yet, through Christ, I believe that God's judgment is a *gracious* judgment. It is therefore crucial that we find ways to bear witness lovingly, joyously, and with a hope that refuses despair.[3] God only knows how much the church needs such witnesses for the living of these days.

1. Now Lambuth University in Jackson, Tennesee, where Gene taught for 45 years.

2. See R. R. Reno, *In the Ruins of the Church: Sustaining Faith in an Age of Diminished Christianity* (Grand Rapids: Brazos, 2002).

3. See Thomas W. Currie, *The Joy of Ministry* (Louisville: Westminster John Knox, 2008). This is a really fine book, especially for discouraged clergy or laity.

John 10:1–18: The Good Shepherd

It is not uncommon to find in church sanctuaries stained glass windows portraying Jesus as a shepherd. In some of these scenes, Jesus is carrying a lamb in one arm and a staff in his other hand. In the background, other sheep are following him. It depicts Jesus leading his sheep to green pastures and to still waters. In these windows, Jesus is the shepherd of Psalm 23.

When I served a congregation with such a stained glass window more than twenty years ago, I confess I was a bit bothered by the scene. After all, I had been trained in the modern manner of reading the Bible historically. I had listened to advocates of modern critical methods who held to their cardinal rule that we cannot read Jesus back into the Old Testament. While even now I do not look for Jesus beneath every Hebrew rock and stump, I do thank God that I have begun to recover from that grave theological error. In a word, I am no longer disturbed by shepherd windows found in a number of churches. If Christ is truly Lord of his Scripture, then it is perfectly legitimate to read Psalm 23 in light of Christ and, conversely, to understand Christ in light of Psalm 23.

That said, we have to be careful not to confuse John 10 with Psalm 23. The two passages are very different. In John 10, Jesus calls himself "the Good Shepherd" (vv. 11, 14).[4] However, Jesus makes no mention of green pastures or of still waters or of souls being restored (Ps 23:2). He does not mention a table being prepared in the presence of enemies (v. 5); he says nothing of walking through the valley of the shadow of death, unafraid (v. 4). Jesus describes the life of his sheep and his care for them very differently than the well-known psalm ascribed to David.

Note three aspects of Jesus' depiction of the flock in John 10. First, there is division within the flock. We cannot be sure of the causes or history of these divisions in the first century, but for purposes of this essay, we can say simply that Jesus has "other sheep that do not belong to this fold" (v. 16). Second, the sheep face internal threats. There is a "hired hand" who lives and works among the flock.[5] The hired hand is not the true shepherd and does not own the sheep (v. 12). He "sees the wolf coming and leaves the sheep and runs away. . . . The hired hand runs

---

4. All Scripture references will be from the New Revised Standard Version.

5. The reference to "strangers" in v. 5 may well need to be included here as a possible reference to similar problems within the church.

away because a hired hand does not care for the sheep" (vv. 12–13). The hired hand fails the sheep in their time of need. And third, the sheep face serious external threats. They suffer the danger of thieves and bandits (v. 8), as well as wolves (v. 12). To summarize: the sheep are experiencing estrangement from other sheep, they are facing internal threats from misleading hired hands, and they are facing external threats that can destroy them. Such is Jesus' description of the life of his sheep.

Though few of us have any direct experience with sheep, we know enough, if only by hearsay, to be sobered by the scene Jesus portrays. To think of sheep who are divided, who must live with hired hands who do not care for them as a shepherd should, and who must contend with wolves and thieves, is altogether frightening. Theirs is a chaotic, perilous, and threatened existence. It is all the more sobering to consider that Jesus is describing the life of his followers in the first century, and that through his Holy Spirit he is describing the ongoing life of his church for the duration of the church's existence. Yet we in the church should be not surprised by Jesus' teaching. We know that denominational struggles and congregational life resonate much more with John 10 than Psalm 23.[6] We do well, therefore, to reflect upon John 10 a bit further.

The Good Shepherd in Light of Ezekiel and Zechariah

Jesus' teaching in John 10 must be heard chiefly in light of the shepherding texts in Ezekiel 34 and Zechariah 10 and 11.[7] The shepherding image is polyvalent. Both Ezekiel and Zechariah will speak of God as a shepherd. Yet, both will also cry out against human shepherds, who are leaders of God's people, who fail in their God-anointed responsibility. Let us keep

6. I suspect that few are the sermons on Good Shepherd Sunday, the fourth Sunday of Easter—or other days when John 10 is the text for preaching—that take with utmost seriousness the scene portrayed by Jesus.

7. The whole of Ezekiel 34; Zechariah 10:2–3; 11:3–17; 13:7. Raymond Brown says it well: "In any use of Jesus of Old Testament figures there is originality; to deny Old Testament background because a new dimension or orientation has been given to Old Testament ideas and symbols is to fail to understand Jesus' relation to the Old Testament. Therefore, the question must not be whether Jesus' symbolism is exactly the same as that of Ezekiel or of other parts of the Old Testament, but whether there is enough similarity to suggest that the Old Testament supplied the raw material for his creative reinterpretation and the continuation of that reinterpretation in the preaching of the apostles." *The Gospel According to John I–XII*, Anchor Bible (Garden City, NY: Doubleday, 1966) 397–98.

in mind, too, that Ezekiel is a sixth-century prophet who lives into the time of the Babylonian exile, whereas Zechariah lives near the end of the sixth century, when the Jews have returned from Exile and are trying to rebuild Jerusalem.[8] Clearly, Jesus is drawing from texts rooted in the exilic and post-exilic experiences of Israel in order to describe the life of his church. Through Christ, these particular shepherding passages in Ezekiel and Zechariah become prophecies about the church's life. They prefigure the dangers that from time to time will befall the body of Christ. We can therefore review the exilic and post-exilic experiences of God's people that are the background for Ezekiel and Zechariah. We will be able to understand more fully what Jesus is teaching in John 10 and will hear more clearly the Word and work of Christ in the contemporary church.

The Experience of Exile

For this review, I am indebted to the work of an Episcopalian priest, Ephraim Radner.[9] Radner identifies three important aspects of the exile and early post-exile. First, the exile and the centuries leading up to it bring about the destruction of the unity of the people of God. We need only briefly to rehearse the story of that broken unity: a unity achieved under David but lost after Solomon's death; the division into northern and southern kingdoms; the gradual loss of tribal identity with even further unraveling of God's people in the centuries that follow; and the final dispersion of the northern tribes at the hand of Assyria and the destruction of Jerusalem and Judah by the Babylonian army. Both the loss of visible unity and the destruction of the people of God are God's judgment upon his people for their deliberate refusal to love one another and to serve him.

8. Though the prophecies near the end of Zechariah may well be the work of a later prophet, canonically speaking, the shepherding passages are associated with Zechariah and with those early post-exilic difficulties.

9. Radner has reflected extensively on the strange and trying ecclesial situation that we face. For this essay, see especially his "The Cost of Communion: A Meditation on Israel and the Divided Church," in *Inhabiting Unity: Theological Perspectives on the Proposed Lutheran-Episcopal Concordat*, eds. Ephraim Radner and R. R. Reno (Grand Rapids: Eerdmans, 1995) 134–52. Other books by Radner: *Hope Among the Fragments: The Broken Church and Its Engagement of Scripture* (Grand Rapids: Brazos, 2004) and the theologically devastating *The End of the Church: A Pneumatology of Christian Division in the West* (Grand Rapids: Eerdmans, 1998).

Second, exilic and post-exilic experience leads Israel toward the formation of a remnant, "not simply in terms of her reduced numbers, but more especially as pertaining to the actual character of her faith."[10] The righteousness of the people and its leaders becomes crucial, because identity within Israel is no longer to be gauged or claimed by one's tribal ancestry. The history of Israel's twelve tribes is never forgotten, but the identity forged out of the exile is one of intramural unity for the sake of Israel's survival and, even more, her witness. Israel's identity begins to be defined in terms of those practices and forms of life that distinguish the people of God from surrounding cultures. We note the oft-mentioned example of Ezra's putting an end to the practice of inter-marriage with those who are not children of Israel. We should see this as but one step taken toward a renewed submission to Torah, around which the remnant is formed.

Third, there is a long-term, unending penitence that contributes to the posture of God's people after the exile. Penitence becomes a part of Jewish character. Books such as Ezra and Nehemiah call the people to repentance, and the people respond with weeping and acts of penitence. The children of Israel's hearts are broken by what has happened to their life as the people of God. In addition, they come to understand, as the years pass, that their exile does not end with their return to Jerusalem. Penitence thus becomes a part of their ongoing communal character and life.

The Experience of Exile Today

The above review of Jewish exilic and post-exilic experiences parallels our experiences in these difficult days of the church. First, we are witnessing the loss, the unraveling, of the unity of the people of God. We are now enduring the divine wrath of disunity—God's wrath being God's willingness to turn us over to our own desires and actions that lead to our modern-day aloofness toward the church at best, and to schism at worst (Rom 1:24, 26, 28).[11] Instances of our failures as the people of God

10. Radner, "Cost of Communion," 146.

11. "I have poured out my indignation upon them; I have consumed them with the fire of my wrath; I have returned their conduct upon their heads, says the Lord God" (Ezek 22:31), as one of many such verses indicating, along with Romans 1, an important aspect of the nature of divine wrath and judgment.

to love one another in these recent generations and centuries are beyond our numbering. The result has been a shattering of the body of Christ, a splintering that cannot be whitewashed by Pollyannaish language in denominational self-promotion. Nor can efforts to develop the anemic doctrines of diversity and inclusiveness overcome the divisions.[12] The body of Christ, to borrow an image from Gerhard Lohfink, is now like "a broken mirror that distorts the image of Christ,"[13] with denominations and traditions seeking to justify their own existence as viable churches, independent of others. A separatist logic is found within every denomination, as we continue to declare what is *unique* about our particular ecclesial tradition. There should be little surprise that such self-justifying logic resists unity with other traditions.[14] We note as well the danger of

12. A worthwhile question tangential to this essay is whether "diversity" and "inclusiveness" are theological terms anyway. Yet they are indeed major influences in the "working theology" within many of our denominations. See Ephraim Radner and Philip Turner, *The Fate of Communion: The Agony of Anglicanism and the Future of a Global Church* (Grand Rapids: Eerdmans, 2006) 243–51.

13. *Does God Need the Church?: Toward a Theology of the People of God*, trans. Linda M. Maloney (Collegeville, MD: Liturgical, 1999) 298. The full quote: "And yet the thesis that all separations can simply be explained and even transfigured as the 'richness of variety' not only contains a highly dangerous element; it is also unbiblical. The condition of Christianity at the present time is nothing like a colorful field in which wheat is growing and poppies and cornflowers are blooming; it is rather like a broken mirror that distorts the image of Christ." And a similar image is employed by John Wilkins who writes about the efforts of the Archbishop of Canterbury, Rowan Williams, to steer the Anglican Communion away from schism: "Constantly Williams has warned that if a smash-up comes, there can be no such thing as a clean break. It will be more like a man putting his fist through a window pane. The fissures will be of every imaginable shape and complexity, and will run predictably in every direction." In *National Catholic Reporter,* September 14, 2007: http://ncronline.org/NCR_Online/ archives2/2007c/ 091407/091407a.php.

14. Lesslie Newbigin, *The Household of God* (New York: Friendship, 1954) contrasts the present situation of the church in the West with that which the Reformers faced in the sixteenth century. The Reformers take Christendom for granted. Newbigin writes, "This means that in their doctrines of the Church they are defining their position over against one another *within* the context of the *corpus Christianum*. They are not defining the Church as over against a pagan world" (2, italics are Newbigin's). In contrast, the church in the West is now in "a missionary situation" in which "Christian disunity [is] an intolerable anomaly. . . . When the Church faces out toward the world, it knows that it only exists as the first-fruits and the instrument of that reconciling work of Christ, and that division within its own life is a violent contradiction of its own fundamental nature. His reconciling work is one, and we cannot be His ambassadors reconciling the world to God, if we have not ourselves been willing to be reconciled to one another. It is the result of this deep connection at the heart of the Gospel itself that Churches which—within Christendom—had accepted their disunity as a matter of course, found that when they

schism within our denominations. In some traditions, schism may already have occurred *de facto*, even if formal *de jure* actions or steps have not been taken. Last, we know all too well of declining denominational allegiance and identity, which is ever so similar to the loss of identity of the tribes of Israel. In a word, the body of Christ is suffering disunity and dispersion not unlike the Diaspora suffered by both Israel and Judah. Moreover, barring a fresh work of the Holy Spirit, we are headed toward a further fracturing of Christian witness in the western world. Like Israel, our unity is being destroyed before our very eyes.

Second, like Israel, we are witnessing and undergoing the painful, gradual formation of a remnant. We should perhaps note that remnant theology is very dangerous, that we are always tempted to think that we belong to the faithful remnant and that those who disagree with us are outside the fold. I would suggest that, given our present ecclesial state, no one can claim to belong to a holy remnant, for we do not know which fragments of the broken body God will use—if God uses any of them. Yet noting the danger of remnant theology does not give us license to ignore this work that God accomplished in Israel and that God is carrying out in the contemporary church. Simply, a remnant is being formed, and obedience constrains us to embrace this revealed manner of God's renewing the life of his people. A remnant ecclesiology assumes holiness, or a distinctive "set-apartness" from the dominant culture that is external to the church. Wherever we may stand, for example, in the unwinnable arguments over the hot-button issues of sexuality and violence, we can note for purposes of this essay that they are debates over holiness. We face other holiness issues as well. Either we will find a way to address the wide range of holiness issues in our life as the church, or God will force them upon us. In a word, God is pressing his people toward holiness and a remnant existence, just as God pressed Israel toward such a life.

Third, as in Israel's history, God is leading the church into a spirit of penitence. A story can help here. A few years ago, my wife and I attended a wedding in another state. As long-time friends of the groom and his family, we attended the customary "rehearsal dinner" the night before the wedding. That evening, I had a significant conversation with the brother of the groom who was raised in a very devout United Methodist home. I

---

were placed in a missionary situation their disunity was an intolerable scandal" (8–9). Though writing in the context of the ecumenical movement and its stirrings more than fifty years ago, Newbigin's insights warrant our reflection.

asked this young man about his life in the church. He responded that he had "given up on traditional Christian faith," that he no longer had regard for the greatest portion of the church's doctrine. He said he liked Jesus, but he did not like what the church has done to Jesus. And, as an artist, he now worshiped as he painted on the canvas. His church was his art. As I listened to him, I wondered how I should respond. I listened in silence; I had to accept his words in sorrow. I saw no need to repudiate what he had to say or to belittle his perspective. I had little choice but to bear in penitence his word of judgment upon the church. This young man had been raised in the gospel life by parents any pastor would want in his or her congregation. Yet the church never captured his heart and mind and life. While it is indeed possible that he may have been driven away from the church because he, like the rich man who met Jesus,[15] saw something of the gospel's radical demands upon his life, it is more likely that he drifted away because his church somehow failed to form him in the beauty, glory, and power of the gospel. How else could I respond in the presence of that young man than in silence to cry to God to have mercy upon us?[16] We who are in the church must be willing to bear graciously such comments when we hear them. We must allow that such disregard for the church is part of God's judgment upon us for our mediocrity and for our diminishing practices of discipleship.

Words like that young man's can be heard at every turn: as we hear of younger adults who leave our churches for other denominations or who leave our churches only to wander with no ecclesial home; as we read each year of our denominations' declining membership numbers, knowing that the best theological minds and most devout evangelical hearts have not been able to reverse the precipitous decline; and as those same membership numbers reveal that worship attendance in many denominations is declining at a faster rate than official membership, a fact which can only be interpreted to mean that life in faith communities is becoming less and less a part of the lives of the people who remain in them. As the Jews were pressed, so we are being pressed toward a posture of penitence as a part of our ongoing communal life in the church.

---

15. Mark 10:17–22.

16. Our conversation was seasoned with the grace of mutual respect for one another. I hasten to add that I offered words of testimony regarding Jesus and his church. Yet my first response was to bear his judgment. This is my point.

Moving toward a summary, these three aspects of disunity, of remnant-forming, and of penitence that we find in our present context are not mere institutional indicators that sociologists can identify. That is to say, they are not simply markers of tired, weary institutions that can be measured by statistics or questionnaires or various studies mandated by church bureaucrats.[17] Rather, they are biblical *prefigurements*. They are prefigured in the exilic and post-exilic experiences of Israel. They are prophesied in Scripture as the way that God brings judgment upon his people with the purpose of renewing his people. The sweeping story of the Old Testament is that the painful experiences of the exile and post-exile finally lead to Jesus Christ. God in providence presses Israel toward the day of her salvation in Christ—a day when the exile "is finished" (John 19:30). Our hope and assurance is that what happened to Israel as accounted in Scripture is happening to us in the cruciform providence of God. In this light, our present church situation is a part of God's ongoing, providential leading of his church toward Christ for the sake of its renewal and witness. Like Israel, our experiences are being taken by Christ into his death. As difficult as it may be for us to see and believe, God's judgment is therefore a gracious judgment. Our present tribulations remain within the grasp of God's unseen hand. And, we are a people of hope even yet, for the church as part of the historical continuation of Israel belongs to God whose gifts and calling are irrevocable (Rom 11:29).

---

17. What can be called the biblical contours of division, of remnant-making, and of ongoing penitence must not become secondary to movements that appear in the church's life. The diverse and varied movements of the past few generations—feminist movements, liberation movements, church growth movements, conservative movements as well as their progressive counterparts, liturgical movements, etc.—can certainly arise in the wisdom of God to bless the church for a while and to assure us that the church is yet a part of the Israel of God. Every movement can become for a season a means of grace, just as Josiah's reforms in Judah were a glimmer of light in the midst of God's unrelenting judgment. Yet these movements must not become the bellwethers for the church's identity or mission. These movements are not new categories of truth or self-understanding. They must not become substitutes for the contours that we find in Scripture. These and other contours will abide long after the present movements have arisen and then passed away to make room for other movements. It is one thing to learn from and delight in any of the renewal movements that come our way. It is quite another thing to hitch the church's wagon to any of them.

The Good Shepherd

It may seem that I have labored too long in the exilic and post-exilic experiences of Israel and of the contemporary church. Yet, I hope it is becoming clear that I have worked to offer an extended reflection upon John 10, where Jesus' followers struggle with disunity, with internal threats, and with external dangers. John 10 resonates with these other voices in Scripture, and it resounds throughout our present life in the church.

We can now move toward the ultimate affirmation found in John 10. Namely, there is a Good Shepherd! This Good Shepherd is at work in his church. He takes into his death the chaos and confusion that beset us. By the willful, loving laying down of his life (vv. 11, 15, 17, 18), the long-endured exile does indeed come to an end. His death becomes the center of his people's life—his death holding us together, even if it is by the skin of our teeth. He works graciously to resist and overcome our internal divisions. He exposes our false shepherding, our unwillingness to give our lives for one another. And, he is working to empower his community to resist the external threats posed by our culture.

I repeat, this Good Shepherd in love lays down his life for the sheep. No one takes his life from him (v. 18). He is the heart of our communal life. His willful self-giving to the point of death is worthy of our imitation. His cross is a mystery inviting our participation, our communion (*koinonia* in Greek). We thus commune with Christ and one another when we embrace the unity he has won for us, when we resist divisions and refuse schism, when we acknowledge his remnant-making work by seeking to develop a "rule of life" that enhances a holiness and righteousness that visibly contrasts with our surrounding culture, and when we make room in the church for penitence, lamentation, and weeping. It goes without saying that we do not relieve ourselves of Jesus' shepherding work by delegating his ministry to those we set apart as our "pastors," our "shepherds." Rather, this cruciform ministry of the Good Shepherd is to be both received and practiced by all who belong to him, as we seek to "outdo one another in showing honor" (Rom 12:10). Our common life is to be "the canvas upon which the crucified Christ . . . [is] publicly displayed."[18]

---

18. Basil S. Davis, "The Meaning of *proegraphe* in the Context of Galatians 3.1," *New Testament Studies* 45 (1999) 194–212; 208. Quoted in Michael J. Gorman, *Cruciformity: Paul's Narrative Spirituality of the Cross* (Grand Rapids: Eerdmans, 2001) 31.

Conclusion

This book rightly names Gene Davenport as a courageous witness to the Gospel of Jesus Christ. When we think of courageous witnesses, we usually think of women and men who stand in the tradition of the prophets. Yet, I do not think of Gene as an Amos or Jeremiah, though others may be so inclined. I am more likely to regard him as being of the "house and lineage"[19] of Ezra. With courage and resilience, Gene has devoted his life to the study of Scripture within today's broken church. For forty-five years, he has asked college students—not to mention Christians and Jews in their congregational settings—to open the Bible, to read it together, and to listen for the Word of God. He has battled modern theological formulations and hermeneutics that make us suspicious of Scripture as the authoritative witness to the ways of God with his church and in his world.[20]

I conclude this essay with a word drawn from the days of Ezra and Nehemiah. Gene no doubt would agree that we find in it a prophecy,[21] a prefigurement of Christ, that gives us important clues for how we are to live "amidst the melancholy of these days" (Calvin). The book of Nehemiah begins:

> The words of Nehemiah son of Hacaliah. In the month of Chislev, in the twentieth year, while I was in Susa the capital, one of my brothers, Hanani, came with certain men from Judah; and I asked them about the Jews that survived, those who had escaped the captivity, and about Jerusalem. They replied, "The survivors there in the province who escaped captivity are in great trouble and shame; the wall of Jerusalem is broken down, and its gates have been destroyed by fire." When I heard these words I sat down and wept, and mourned for days, fasting and praying before the God of heaven (Neh. 1:1–4).

Then Nehemiah does a remarkable thing. As cupbearer for King Artaxerxes, he goes to the king, and asks the king for permission to re-

---

19. Luke 2:4 (KJV).

20. His scorn for the way his own United Methodist tradition has bowed to our latterly configured "Wesleyan quadrilateral" of Scripture, tradition, reason, and experience—often rendering Scripture little more than "first among equals"—is but one example of his lifelong effort to call the church to the Bible.

21. A central text in Reno's book.

turn to Jerusalem. He wants to return to the ruins, to stand where the gates once stood. He commits himself to the recovery of the broken and fallen city of God. Nehemiah desires to live among the ruins of Judah. Surely Nehemiah's love for a fallen Judah prefigures the crucifixion of Jesus who pours out his life for a fallen and ruined Israel. Nehemiah's love is a prophetic anticipation of the cruciform love seen in the Good Shepherd who gives his life for a church whose stones are scattered and whose gates are burning.

We see in Nehemiah a foretaste of the ecclesial love to which we are called. As Nehemiah lives among the rubble of Jerusalem, so we are to live in the rubble of a church that we love, with absolutely no idea what the future will be, but trusting that the church is even yet in the hands of the Good Shepherd. This Good Shepherd continues to lay down his life for the sheep in the very congregations in which we make our homes. We can give our lives to the church,[22] trusting that God is pressing us toward his Son in God's providential wisdom. We can pray with the psalmist (102:12–14): "But you, O Lord, are enthroned forever; your name endures to all generations. You will rise and have compassion on Zion; for it is time to favor it; the appointed time has come. For your servants hold its stones dear, and have pity on its dust."[23]

---

22. It has been said that we have no need to fear loving the church too much, so long as our Christology is higher than our ecclesiology.

23. Referenced as the last lines in Radner's *The End of the Church* (354).

Blinded by the Light: A Sermon

Stanley Hauerwas

It may seem odd to use a sermon in a *Festschrift* to honor an academic, but then Gene Davenport is no mere academic. He has always brought to his work a passion for the gospel that is anything but "normal" for an academic. Gene is not as well known as he should be, thus my statement that Gene and Jo Jones are the best unknown theologians in America.

In his book *Into the Darkness,* he states:

> The language of Darkness is metaphor only in the sense that all human language is metaphor. Because God is transcendent, even our language about God is metaphor. Unfortunately, however, most of Western society today has lost any sense of God as transcendent. This is not to say that our problem is, as was said a few years ago, a loss of a sense of Transcendence as such. There *is* no such thing as Transcendence, for Transcendence is an attribute of certain "realities," not a reality unto itself. The problem of Western society is not a loss of a "sense of transcendence" or a loss of a "sense of mystery," as though these were larger categories under which to subsume the figure of God. Our problem is atheism.[1]

Here we see a theologian of extraordinary words, reminding us that the issue is not Transcendence—but God. Gene Davenport, in every word of *Into the Darkness*, understands that transcendence names the idolatry contrary to Christian worship of Jesus of Nazareth. I hope the following sermon indicates the kind of training Gene Davenport suggests we must undergo today if we are to rightly see the world in which we live. For it is a world that calls the darkness light. In this sermon, I try to help us learn how to avoid being blinded by the light.

1. *Into the Darkness: Discipleship in the Sermon on the Mount* (Nashville: Abingdon, 1988) 34.

≈

1 SAMUEL 16:1–13
PSALM 23
EPHESIANS 5:8–14
JOHN 9:1–41

The story I learned in school, the story that has shaped the world in which you and I live, in broad outline goes like this: we are the climax; we have inherited the achievements of a succession of civilizations. From the Hebrews we learned to leave behind polytheism and most forms of religious superstition. From the Greeks we have been taught the power of reason through the development of philosophy and the beginnings of science. These achievements were given new power by Christians who, drawing on both Jewish and Greek sources, transformed the Roman Empire to create what we now call Western civilization.

Unfortunately, this story of progress was side tracked for centuries by what is called the Middle Ages or, more pejoratively, the Dark Ages. During those dark times the human spirit was suppressed by an authoritarian religious regime that legitimated repressive forms of political rule. But with the Reformation, the freedom essential to human development was rediscovered. That freedom found political expression through the American and French revolutions.

The pivotal moment in these developments is called the Enlightenment. This name marks the time, a time beginning with the eighteenth century, in which we learned, in the words of Kant's famous slogan, to "have the courage to use our own reason." Through the use of reason, moreover, we have found the means to free ourselves from the limits of nature, disease, and death.

America is the name that sums up these developments. We are the society and the politics, a democratic politics, which exemplifies this birth of human freedom, this movement from darkness to light. We are, as it says on the dollar, *novus ordo seclorum*, the New Order of Ages. As Americans we are aware that we have yet to be all we should like to be, but we are confident that if any people deserve the description, "enlightened," it is the American people.

Our enlightened status is only confirmed because we understand that the story I have told is far too simple. For example, we know that not everything about the Dark Ages was dark. We know the Greeks as well as many of those identified with the Enlightenment had slaves. Yet, our ability to identify the wrongs of the past assumes the broad outline of the story I have told is true. We simply cannot imagine living in any other world.

That is certainly true for me. I may be a theologian, but I am an academic. That means I am a servant of that great institution of the Enlightenment—the university. Even though I am a theologian, many assume my task is to show that what we believe as Christians is not incompatible with the story of the Enlightenment. For example, I know the power the story I have told has on my life by my response to the question the disciples ask: "Rabbi, who sinned, this man or his parents, that he was born blind?" I am a representative of the Enlightenment. I know the answer to that question: no one sinned—he was just born blind.

I should like to think that Jesus anticipates my enlightened response to his disciples' question because he refuses to accept the premise that this man's blindness had anything to do with sin. But, unfortunately, he rejects that premise for reasons that are even more offensive to my enlightened sensibilities than the suggestion that this man's blindness might be due to sin. Jesus says that this man was born blind so that God's work might be revealed in him. I am embarrassed by the suggestion that anyone was born blind, reduced to begging, in order that Jesus might show he had the power to heal. It is all well and good for Jesus to claim that "he is the light of the world," but he could have said that without this man's blindness.

That I have this response, as I suspect many of you do as well, to the story of the man born blind is an indication of the hold the story with which I began has on our lives. Does this mean we should rethink our assumption that we stand in the light? Could it possibly be the case that I am, that we are, blinded by the light? Could it be that the story I have told, the story I suspect grips you as it grips me, makes it impossible for us to see Jesus? How could that be? Are we not the most enlightened people the world has ever known? Surely if anyone can see Jesus, it must be people like us? I suspect, like Samuel trying to choose the king from Jesse's sons, we assume we would know what a king or savior should look like. But we do not see kings, saviors, or the world just by looking. Rather, Jesus claims, we learn what it might mean for the world to be saved by learning to see him.

Learning to see Jesus entails a training that challenges our presumption that we are already in the light. The man born blind is able to see Jesus because he had the advantage of being born blind. We fail to see Jesus because we have the disadvantage of being enlightened. It turns out, moreover, that we cannot will our way out of our enlightened darkness. Rather, we must be confronted by a light so brilliant that we are able to see the darkness our pride mistakes as light. An extraordinary claim, but what do you expect? We are Christians after all. We worship a crucified God—that takes some getting used to.

We were told at the very beginning of the Gospel of John that the light would shine in the darkness, but the darkness would not overcome it. Now we begin to understand that the darkness does not know itself as darkness until it encounters the light. This is why we are loath to give up the darkness, because we cannot imagine what it would mean to live in the light of Christ. Ask yourself, for example, what might it mean to see those born blind, to see those desperately ill, to see those in inexplicable suffering in the light of Christ? We must submit to being overcome by Christ's light in order to see the darkness that presently blinds us.

Everyone in our scripture for today finds it hard to see rightly what Jesus has done. After the blind man comes back from washing his eyes in the pool of Siloam, many of his neighbors are unsure if he is the same beggar they knew had been blind from birth. He insists he is the same man, but the account he gives for how his eyes were opened only seems to make it more difficult to confirm that he is the same one who was born blind. Moreover, he is not of much help because he is not even sure who healed him or where the one who restored his sight might be. He may be able to see, but he remains in the dark. Healed of his blindness, he will have to undergo training if he is to see Jesus.

The training begins by his attempt to respond to the Pharisees' questions about how he had received his sight as well as how it could be that he had been healed on the Sabbath. The man born blind resorts to the most readily available theological theory that could explain who it is that has healed him: "He is a prophet." But the Pharisees have an equally plausible response. Jesus cannot be a prophet. Prophets are from God. They do God's will. But Jesus, if in fact he healed the blind man, healed him on the Sabbath. So he cannot be a prophet.

Some who seem to have a more empirical bent doubt if he was ever blind. They confront his parents with the not-so-subtle suggestion that they may have lied about their son's blindness. His parents stubbornly maintain he was born blind but refuse to take sides about how or who opened his eyes. Because his parents fear they will lose their good standing in the synagogue, they put the responsibility on their son—"He is of age: ask him."

The man born blind is called a second time before the sagacious class of his day. They demand that he acknowledge that Jesus must be a sinner. The man whose sight has been restored is beginning to learn. He states what he knows. It is not for him to say whether Jesus is or is not a sinner. What he knows, however, is that he was blind, but now he sees. His accusers press the issue. They want to know how his sight was restored. They demand an explanation. The man born blind recognizes he has nothing to lose. He even resorts to irony, asking if those who doubt he has been healed want to hear the story again in order that they might become a disciple of Jesus.

Irony, however, is seldom a weapon that persuades an adversary, particularly an adversary who is more powerful, because their power derives from the presumption that they represent what "everyone knows." So the man born blind is reviled by those who claim to possess true knowledge, the knowledge that comes from Moses, and everyone knows God spoke to Moses. The man-born-blind's argumentative skills, however, are increasing. He counters their argument about Moses, pointing out that God does not listen to sinners but to those who worship and obey God's will. Then, in an extraordinary theological move, he observes that since the world began no one born blind has had their eyes opened. That his eyes have been opened must, therefore, indicate that the one who healed him is from God. Indeed, it may be that Jesus is not only from God, but shares in God's very life. Such a suggestion is too much for those who think they have the knowledge of Moses. They have had enough. They resort to the first mode of explanation—"You who were born in sin are trying to teach us?" They throw him out of the synagogue.

The man born blind still does not know where Jesus might be, but Jesus, hearing of his excommunication, seeks him out. Jesus recognizes that the man he has healed has now undergone the training necessary to recognize who he is. So he asks him: "Do you believe in the Son of Man?" The formerly blind man is ready to believe, but he is not sure who the Son of Man might be. Jesus' response is telling, "You have seen him." In saying this, Jesus is affirming what the blind man has otherwise not been given permission to acknowledge, namely, that Jesus is from God. Jesus, the Son of Man, now stands before the man born blind. The man not only says, "Lord, I believe," but we are told, "He worshiped him." The blind man is a good Jew. You can only worship God. This man, this blind man, has finally learned to see Jesus.

Jesus then makes clear what has been clear from the beginning of this extraordinary episode—he has come into the world that those who do not see may see, and those who do see may become blind. Some of the Pharisees hearing this ask, rhetorically, if Jesus meant to suggest they might be blind. Jesus responds that because they think they see, because they assume they are already in the light, they remain blinded by the light.

Given the alternatives, if we had to identify with anyone in this narrative, most of us I suspect would choose to be the man born blind. But remember our reaction to Jesus' statement that this man had been born blind in order that God's work might be revealed in him. Even after we have been healed by Jesus, I suspect most of us could not help but feel a bit misused. Which again is a reminder of what a radical transformation is required—particularly for those of us who pride ourselves on being enlightened—if we are to see Jesus as the very Son of Man and Son of God.

Paul writes to the Ephesians reminding them that they were once in darkness, but now they are "in the Lord," which means, Paul says, "You are the light." As children of the light we are to bear fruit, because the light is found in all that is good, right, and true. Paul then urges the Ephesians to try to find what is pleasing to the Lord by doing nothing in secret that cannot be made visible to the whole church. For it is through such a process, a process that can never be finished, that we discover what is pleasing to the Lord for our time and place.

Such a process, such a training, is required if we are to discern what is good, what is right, what is true about our story of enlightenment. I am not suggesting that everything about that story is evil, wrong, or false. Rather, I am suggesting that as those shaped by that story we are going to need all the help we can get if we are to discern, as Paul argues we must, what it means to live in the light of Jesus and to be that light for the world. The great challenge is not how we can fit Jesus into the story of Enlightenment, but how the story of the Enlightenment is to be judged by Jesus.

For let us confess that this story, our self-congratulatory story, of our enlightened status can make it difficult for us to see and worship Jesus. We want Jesus to confirm what we have learned from a world that cannot believe that the Father would redeem the world through the gift of the Son. The world in which we live would tempt us to believe that our prayers for healing are only meant to show that we care for one another. The world in which we live would have us describe the bread and wine of the Eucharist as symbols, but not the reality of the body and blood of Jesus.

If we are to be the light of Christ, we must have our lives illumined by those Christians who have other stories to tell than the story we tell of our enlightened status as Americans. We will only learn to see Jesus if we learn to listen to how their vision has been shaped by their speech. To undergo such training will be painful and will require great patience. It may be as hard and demanding as trying to understand one of Ugandan Anglican Bishop Ochola's stories or what it means for Haitian Christians to engage in the slow, hard work of building a school.

I do not know how our learning to listen to the stories of Christians in different times and places will change our story. I do not know what it will mean for the kind of education we give our children. I do not know what it will mean for how we understand ourselves as Americans. I do not know what it will mean for how we negotiate a world in which the means we use to gain control of fate and death make us ever more fated by our own creations. But I do know we will only begin to know how to answer such questions if, like the man born blind, we learn to see and worship Jesus.

Telling and Hearing Our Stories in Communities of Grace

Billy Vaughan

Asked to write on his greatest pain and how it had shaped his experience of "call," Marlon Foster shared the story of his friend Pierre's death. They were more than friends, he insisted; they were brothers. Throughout middle school, they were inseparable. At seventeen, they moved into an apartment together. At eighteen Marlon watched his friend, his brother, Pierre, die from a bullet wound to the head. It was a bullet that could just as easily have struck Marlon. At the time of Pierre's death, he and Marlon made money by selling drugs. Like a host of other young African American teenagers in their urban neighborhood, they lived on the brink of death day in and day out.

When Marlon shared this story, it was, simultaneously, his story of pain and of call. I, along with twelve of his fellow seminarians, sat silently as he read. We heard about the dramatic turn that his life took following Pierre's death—how he graduated from college and afterwards faced corporate offers and dreams that typically meant moving away from the old neighborhood forever. But each new morning brought memories of Pierre. The pain simply did not go away with time.

Marlon's pain didn't and wouldn't ease until he made the commitment to stay in the neighborhood and begin a ministry called "Knowledge Quest," a ministry reaching out to the hosts of children and youth in the neighborhood who, like Marlon and Pierre, both wanted and needed a better road than gangs, guns and drugs. Marlon's story, like that of Moses (whose story we had read together through the week), was of a burning fire that would not go out until he said "yes" to his call.

Marlon Foster's story is one of many shared in servant leadership classes at Memphis Theological Seminary. In servant leadership classes, we tell our stories in relationship to themes such as "Being and Becoming

God's Beloved," "Power and the Powers," "Money," "Reconciliation/The Beloved Community," and "Call." We reflect on scriptures that we have shared in common through the week. We respond to various writers who have written provocatively on the above themes. We keep covenants of prayer and service, contemplation and action. But, in the end, we tell our stories and do so in the presence of others, hoping that our stories can and will be woven into the narrative of the Christ. In our better moments, we tell the truth. Whenever we dare to do so it is with the conviction that the Christ has chosen to join us, both in the classroom and, more to the point, in our neighborhoods.

Whenever we tell our stories, we are also, of course, telling the stories of the churches and communities from which we came. In The Servant Leadership School, in groups of six to twelve, we end up sharing much more than ideas; we share the beauty, power, pathos, and struggles of our own, our neighborhoods' and our faith communities' lives in this world.

The Gospel story always takes place amidst the very real and un-predictable, unplanned and sometimes unprecedented stories of people and communities. To speak of practices such as mercy, compassion, reconciliation, justice, and righteousness, without access to the narra-tives of people and communities, is to turn our lives into mere facts and principles that fail to offer the real transformation for which we and our world are crying out.

Sharing his story was more than an exercise in self-expression for Marlon. He needed to tell his story in the context of call. He needed to hear his story in the company of others who honored the particulars of his sacred journey, but also helped him listen more deeply for how his journey fit into the sacred narrative of Jesus Christ—God with us.

Marlon, his wife Sheila, and their three children are now establish-ing even deeper roots in their neighborhood. To his surprise, he and Sheila have recently co-founded a new church (Christ Quest Community Church) that at times includes more neighborhood children than adults.

Ironically, as both Knowledge Quest and the church have expanded, a number of pastors both in and beyond the neighborhood have urged him to move out of the neighborhood, to drive a nicer car, buy a bigger house for him and his family—to lay claim to his "success" in very visible ways. He has often felt the label of "young idealist," and at times wondered if he is crazy for believing that God wants him, his wife and children, to be *in*, not just *for*, the neighborhood.

In a Servant Leadership class, in the company of others who were gathered to tell, hear and interpret their stories, Marlon claimed his journey as one of faith and faithfulness—his own and, more significantly, God's. He re-experienced his call and his deep sense of God's accompaniment. The other participants affirmed, encouraged, and confirmed, but also pressed for greater clarity of this call.

Truthfully, without such contexts for interpreting our stories, most of us drift. Worse than that, we sink deeply into the narrative of the dominant culture. Unfortunately, in our church communities, our pain, gifts, and burning fires are rarely even placed on the table. Rather than being woven into a communal narrative rich with purpose and reflective of the "Body of Christ," we find ourselves embedded in a narrative that is often quite at odds with the Gospel.

~

I was the director of a youth center in Ripley, Tennessee. On the weekends, our youth center was the place to be. We had a pool table, a ping-pong table, music, cards, rap sessions, and loads of youth participating. I should add, we had lots of white youth participating. After all, it was 1975.

Midway through the summer, on a Friday night, three young African American boys came to the center and asked if they could participate. Ironically, this center was in the heart of town and much closer to the homes of these three young guys than to any of the white youth. When they came to the door, everything slowed down. The center grew quiet. Clearly, in the stillness of that moment was the question: "Will you let them in?" I invited them in, and within seconds, the games picked back up. After all, many of these kids knew one another from school. If anything, it was one of our more festive Friday nights. For the next few weeks, black and white youth were together at this Christian youth center—joyfully and without incident.

I was young and naïve. I didn't see it coming. On a Saturday night, the mother of one of the white youth came to pick her daughter up and was "shocked" by what she saw. When I refused her request to send the black youth away she drove to the pastor's house to inform him of this grave situation. Within minutes, the pastor wheeled around the corner in his pickup truck, wearing jeans and a pajama top. He called me outside, away from the crowd and demanded that I send "them" away. When I said that I couldn't and wouldn't, he replied, as if talking to himself, that he supposed I was right, that it was probably illegal. Then, as if possessed by a brilliant idea, he rushed inside, pulled the plug on the music box and announced that everyone *had to leave, that the center was closed for the night.*

The message was loud and clear. One by one the youth filed by, walking by the pastor and me as they exited the center. I have long been haunted by the look on the face of the young African American who two weeks earlier had knocked on the door and asked for permission *to be a youth among youth.*

I followed the pastor to his house. Over the next hour, we engaged in something akin to theological debate. Finally, perhaps simply to be rid of me, he conceded that what he'd done was neither ethical nor of Jesus, but ended this lesson in ecclesiology by saying that "Jesus doesn't pay the bills, the people do." And the people who paid the bills at the church would simply not allow race mixing. I turned in my resignation the next day and left a note on the door of the center saying "closed for the summer."

My deepest pain? Haunting as it was, it was not the look on the face of the young African American boy. My deepest pain was the loss of the church that night. In a very real sense, I had grown up with two clearly-identified "loyalties" in my life—the nation and the church. By this time in my young life, I had already faced the loss of nation as an unambiguous good. Being in Memphis during the sanitation strike and the assassination of Dr. King, coming of age in the midst of Vietnam and Watergate, re-reading history and seeing the genocide of the Native American and the slavery that established the American economy—all had taken away the god-like status with which I had held this nation. But until that night in Ripley I had somehow retained the Church as a kind of god, as a place and a people who, though flawed, were mostly about the will and ways of God in the world. On that night in Ripley, the pastor's words that the people who pay the bills determine our actions in the church ripped from my heart the bedrock that I had counted on in this all-too-chaotic world.

Over the next several months, my life began to come apart at the seams. I was in a car wreck that probably should have killed me. My fiancé and I broke our engagement. On the surface, I managed a strong façade. No one, and I least of all, understood the depth of pain and despair I was experiencing. Six months after leaving Ripley, I crashed. I hit a wall of darkness. Life itself seemed like an illusion.

Looking back, I shudder to think what might have happened during this period had I not been utterly surrounded by family, friends, and mentors who stood with me. They never flinched at my brokenness. They bore the darkness and pain with me. Their love and patience helped me to begin a healing that, in some ways, continues to this day. Paradoxically it was through this experience of pain and despair that I experienced the power of the ecclesiola *(little church) in the midst of the terribly fractured* ecclesia.

⌇

This was *my* story. It was a story I had written and shared in a bit different form in earlier servant leadership classes. In the past, it had always been centered on race and racism, on the haunting pain and, even more, the haunting forgiveness I saw in the look of the African American youth. Those reflections had always led to naming my burning desire to work for both justice and reconciliation in the world.

In this writing, for the first time, I named the loss of the church as my greatest pain. For the first time I also faced my complicity in the racism of the church, admitting that I drove away early the next morning, all too willing to avoid speaking truth to power, i.e., to the people who pay the bills. Ironically, for years, that had been my all-too-easy critique of the pastor.

The questions that Marlon and others asked of me that day were very perceptive—sensitive, for sure, but also searing. Responding to their questions, I began to see clearly an abiding passion for the church that had, in fact, never been lost. I suddenly understood that, in part, my work with the School of Servant Leadership (raising up Christian servant leaders with courage and a depth of faith fit for a culture in the clutches of "empire") had been born out of the pain of my own as well as the pastor's cowardice and lack of faith.

On that day, to my surprise and almost against my will, I also connected my experience of the pastor to a story of conversion that had dogged me for years. It was a story that I'd read, quoted and somewhat sworn by, but never quite understood. It was a story told by a gadfly/mentor/friend, Will Campbell.

In his classic autobiographic book, *Brother to a Dragonfly*, Will Campbell tells of his "conversion" to a Christian faith that he had long been preaching. It took place not in church on Sunday morning, or for that matter in a small group intentionally sharing their faith, but in the home of a somewhat crazy (crazy-like-a-fox) reformer named P. D. East, and in the presence of Will's pharmaceutical-drug-addicted brother. In the company of these two men, Will heard the news of the brutal murder of his friend Jonathan Daniel, a young seminarian who had been working to register black voters in Alabama in the early sixties.

Months earlier, Will had given the skeptical P. D. East an eight-word definition of the Gospel ("We're all bastards but God loves us anyway"). On the occasion of the tragic death of Will's friend, Jonathan, P. D. decided to force Will's hand on that definition, and in doing so to force Will's hand on his professed Christian faith. "Which bastard did God love more," P. D. asked Will, "your gentle friend Jonathan or that brutal murderer Thomas Coleman?"

Conversions are more than assent to certain doctrines. Repentance, *metanoia*, means a total change of perspective and, more than that, of direction. Will tried to talk around P. D.'s examination, but his crazy teacher wouldn't let him. On that day, Will came face to face with a Gospel that was more revolutionary than the civil rights movement in which he had become a central player. He wept as he confessed and professed from depths that had perhaps always been there but which had been masked by the excitement of the civil rights movement and therefore too little attended. Thomas Coleman *was* loved as deeply by God as the gentle man that Coleman had murdered. The forgiveness and reconciliation that Christ was offering included the Thomas Colemans of this world. On that day, Will's life took a turn that he clearly neither expected nor intended:

> One who understands the nature of tragedy can never take sides. And I had taken sides. Many of us who were interested in racial justice had taken sides and there are good reasons in history for doing what we did. We who left home, or were pushed from home when Mamma or Daddy couldn't understand, were just a little bit prideful of our alienation from them, and a little bit arrogant in our newfound liberation and assumed sophistication. We justified it in terms of the suffering, the injustices, the blatant hostilities and economic deprivations black people had had heaped upon them. There was drama and romance in the Civil Rights Movement, and we who had no home at home sought that home in the black cause. Because we did not understand the nature of tragedy we learned the latest woolhat jokes, learned to cuss Mississippi and Alabama sheriffs, learned to say 'redneck' with the same venomous tones we had heard others, or ourselves, say 'nigger.' We did not understand that those we so vulgarly called 'redneck' were a part of the tragedy. They had been victimized one step beyond the

black. They had had their head taken away by cunning, skillful and well-educated gentlemen and ladies of the gentry.[1]

For over thirty years, I had read these words, again and again and again. I had read them certain of the wisdom and truth they bore, but also, I now know, in hope that I would one day truly understand them. Only in telling and retelling my own story of pain, loss, and call relating to events at Ripley, unable to move on, drawn into telling it one more time (as if in doing so I would discover something that had long eluded me), did I finally see the connections between Thomas Coleman and the pastor who said "Jesus doesn't pay the bills."

This pastor, after all, had been a man of deep faith. He had been filled with Christian conviction, so much so that he committed his life to ministry at a time when the economics and the constant moves that went with the Methodist "itinerancy" could hardly have been called attractive. Seminary educated and sent out, with a large family and bills to pay, he found himself facing, again and again, church institutions engulfed in a culture more shaped by consumer capitalism, individualism and, yes, racism, than in the Gospel he had been prepared to preach.

Dr. Walter Bruggemann, reflecting on the scores of theology students whose faith had faded if not folded under such pressure, once told his friend Gordon Cosby: "We send them out alone, Gordon, and the culture is too strong."[2] More often than not, he told Gordon, within a very few years these students became a shell or shadow of the persons of faith they had been when they left the seminary community.

Clearly, the culture had been too strong for the pastor at Ripley. And even though we Methodists love to pride ourselves on being a "connectional system," the truth is that, for the most part, this pastor *was* sent out alone. The "connectional system" itself was marked more by an ethos of

1. Will D. Campbell, *Brother To a Dragonfly* (New York: Continuum, 1977) 225.

2. This conversation was reported to the writer by Gordon Cosby, the founding pastor of The Church of The Saviour in Washington D.C., and confirmed by Walter Brueggemann. Having experienced the power of Walter's lectures on biblical texts a number of times over the years, insisting that each of Walter's visits and lectures at the Church of The Saviour had led to months' worth of listening and change with their community, Gordon did the math. He estimated the numbers of students and hours of engagement between Walter and seminarians at Eden seminary in St. Louis and Columbia seminary in Atlanta over the span of 25 plus years, and he asked a very pointed and, for Gordon, passionate question: "Is there hope for the church?" Walter replied, immediately, "No Gordon, the culture is too strong. We send them out alone, and . . . ."

upward mobility, of succeeding in smaller churches in order to "arrive" at larger, richer churches, than by real mutual support to preach and practice the Gospel. The courage and support he and others needed were not to be found in district preachers' meetings or coffee shop conversations.

This culture *is* too strong for isolated leaders/pastors. What's more, this culture isn't just around us, but is very much *in* each one of us. How can it be otherwise? In the end, even under the best of circumstances and with extraordinary mentors, do we really believe that a few years of the best and most prophetic higher education can do the trick? During those years, we may *begin* to see outside Plato's cave, but it is typically only a beginning. The journey that keeps us moving between worlds is, to put it lightly, a demanding journey.[3]

If we intend to exorcise the powerful spirits of individualism, consumerism, nationalism, racism, and classism, not to mention the deep roots of chaotic sexuality and violence that have made their way into our blood stream by way of the dominant culture, it will take both spiritual discipline *and* support from a spiritually healthy community. As our Methodist founder, John Wesley insisted, in order to chart the journey between worlds, pastors and laity alike need an *ecclesiola in ecclesia*—a small community whose nature and purpose is to help us see and be faithful to the new culture into which we have been baptized and ordained.

It was in sharing my story of pain and loss in the company of such a small community that I began to understand my own avoidance of the powers, and, for the first time, to have some empathy for a pastor who chose to pull the plug, not simply on some young boys, but also on his own faith. Among these friends in the faith, I began to see more clearly that he was an agent, for sure, but also a victim of institutions and culture that confuse and divide our souls. So am I. So are we all.

Of course, in the end we all tell and hear and interpret our stories in community. It isn't whether we do so, but the nature, ethos, and larger narrative of the community in which we do so that makes the difference. Carlyle Marney, commenting on Romans 8, said that the creation itself is

3. Gene Davenport introduced me to "civil religion," Will Campbell, the writings of William Stringfellow, Jacques Ellul, and Thomas Merton and, in many ways, to the Christian narrative with which I'd grown up. He, along with Charles Mayo, Brady and Emmy Lou Whitehead, and others at Lambuth College (now Lambuth University), "invited" me (a diplomatic way of saying this) to see the world outside of the all too conventional cave to which I had grown accustomed. On my better days, I've forgiven them.

desperately crying out, waiting for the children of God to grow up and act like it. Doing so insists on a god, a narrative, and a community that are up to the task of restoring, rather than simply mirroring, our fractured world.

Our Christian narrative is about a very particular God and a specific kind of community. Our narrative is at once a narrative of grace and a prophetic call. These two, in fact, cannot be separated. This narrative reaches prodigals and outcasts, tax collectors and would-be-heroic disciples who aren't so heroic after all. It engages Pharisees who come in the middle of the night to talk theology, leaders of the synagogue who come in broad daylight because the mark of death is on their children and the synagogue, military leaders who honestly care for those under their authority, but also blind beggars, women with a flow of blood, and, for that matter, even sincere, but sincerely wrong, religious leaders such as Saul who passionately called for blood to flow for followers of "the Way."

This narrative—this God of "the Way"—embraces young men like Marlon and Pierre caught up in the nihilism of gangs and drugs. It reaches out to pastoral leaders who are, at the same time, victims *and* promoters of the systems that create and maintain the despair beneath that nihilism. Our Christian narrative invites to the table young ministerial students who talk bravely but are secretly terrified, as well as deputy sheriffs who are desperate for any form of affirmation and recognition they can find. The prophetic mercy of Christ creates a new table, a new culture, where violence and division, desperation and despair give way to the in-breaking reign of God-With-Us, here and now. In Christ, this very particular God offers reconciliation and hope to a frightened world.

To recognize this, as Will Campbell did in dialogue with an irascible theology teacher, is to entertain a deeper understanding of tragedy, for sure, but it is also to be confronted with a grace worthy of the word *metanoia*. If we are to negotiate this journey between cultures—if we are to live creatively into the ongoing and demanding witness of those who sponsor the reign of God on earth as it is in heaven—we will need this God, this narrative, and the companionship of others who likewise have seen and tasted this new world.

Servant Leadership*

James T. Laney

This is a glorious day for many reasons. It is a glorious day because we welcome a new dean to Candler, Dean Jan Love. It is a glorious day for Emory because Emory reaffirms, by this appointment and by this ceremony, the importance of Candler within the community and the role of the church at Emory. I congratulate Dean Love and the University on a stunning appointment, for its reaffirmation of the central role of Candler here. This is a wonderful occasion and I feel very privileged to be here.

I cannot help but recall my own arrival at Candler thirty-eight years ago. I was very new to Emory and to Atlanta. Emory was a simpler, less ceremonial place then. My installation consisted of handing me the keys to my office. Now that office was a very sacred space. It had been occupied solely by the legendary Dean William R. Cannon from the time the building was built until he left to become bishop. Needless to say, as I arrived early one morning, opening the door and walking in, I felt like an intruder. I sat in the chair at the desk and didn't feel at home. In that moment, the custodian came in and upon seeing me, his face became stricken with alarm. He thought that someone was trespassing on Dean Cannon's space. He said to me, "Does Dean Cannon know you're in his office?" I looked at him somewhat sheepishly and said, "Probably not. Maybe I better call and tell him I'm here and make it official!" I prize

* [Editor's note: this address was given at the inauguration of Dean Jan Love at Candler School of Theology, Emory University. With Dr. Laney's permission, we omitted parts of his greeting and opening comments about Emory, but did not omit the references and examples relating to Candler School of Theology within the speech. To do so, we believe, would be to miss the context and power of the speech. Mark 10:35–45, the biblical text referred to below, guided these reflections on Christian leadership. Dr. Laney's emphasis on the leader as servant fits well with the theme of the book and with the character of the man we honor by way of this book.]

those years at Candler and the colleagues and dear friends we made and cherish still.

Candler stands proudly among the professional schools at Emory. All of these professional schools are recognized for their distinguished faculty, their innovative programs, and their rigorous standards. Their graduates occupy positions of leadership and prominence in their several professions. All professional education moves between two poles: on the one hand, the demands to master the requirements for practice at the highest level of competence and expertise, and on the other, the professional goals, the aims that the whole profession espouses, mainly serving the larger good beyond the interests of the individual professional. Now Emory has become well known in addressing that tension creatively, but whatever the larger course of the common good, a true professional obviously must subordinate the self to the role of addressing the needs of the patient, the client, the parishioner, of avoiding undue subjectivity and not relying entirely on good intentions. The best professionals know what they are doing, and they do it with verve and confidence. The best professionals, in other words, are disciplined into their profession for the highest skills of practice.

Candler shares these characteristics with the other professional schools. Candler has its own set of objective criteria and mastery, competence in ministry in all of its forms, abetted by rigorous scholarship and research. But, unlike other professions, ministry at its heart is more than competence at the highest level. It is more than performative; it seeks to be transformative. That is, it seeks changes in the self, in the church, and in society that are appropriate for the understanding of what God intends for his creation. When I say transformative, I don't mean manipulative or exploitative. I mean transformative in the sense in which the heart at its deepest level speaks to the heart of another. In that inner freedom, the response is a response with authenticity and integrity. This is why within ministry we not only seek the highest competence of our graduates, but also correspondingly to see them in their pilgrimage of faith.

Now to pursue that pilgrimage of faith in seminary means that the faculty have an additional responsibility, if not burden, that is not always welcome. The faculty do not simply teach, supervise, help, advise, and counsel. They also have the opportunity to reflect upon their own pilgrimage as the students experience and reflect upon their journey of faith. It is never something accomplished or polished or finished. The idea is not how far we've come, but that we're on the way. It is precisely in sharing their own reflections with students in moments outside the formalities of the classroom that the faculty can, with their rich experience and rigorous reflection, work to weed out self-indulgence and sentimentalism. This is not antithetical to call or commitment, but seeks to discern within the student as well as within one's self what it is we are called to do and to become.

This is why I chose to begin with this passage from the Gospel of Mark. On the road, Jesus, hearing murmuring and dissension, stops to ask the disciples what they were discussing. They were abashed and embarrassed because they were talking about who would be first. There was a rivalry going on even among those who had left all to follow him. Their commitment wasn't in question. But, among these committed disciples was the question "who is going to be number one?" Maybe number two! No one wants to be number eleven or twelve. Jesus, as he always did, used this as a teaching occasion: "He who would be first must be last and servant of all."

Jesus had, of course, referred to himself many times as a servant. On other occasions when James and John sought the high places in the kingdom, Jesus said much the same thing: "You know how the gentiles, the barbarians, exercise power and lord it over others with their authority, but it shall not be so among you. He who would be truly first must be last and servant of all." Paul in Philippians, in possibly the earliest hymn of the church, advises those he is writing to in Philippi, "Have this mind among you which was in Jesus." Carry yourselves as he did! Have this *bearing* among you, which we know in Jesus, not standing on ceremony or privilege or status. "He did not seek equality with God, but emptied himself, being found as a human being, became a servant, became obedient even unto death." That is the story. God has ratified that servanthood itself is the way to go, not only for Jesus, but for every one of us as well.

Therefore, in our theological studies, when we talk about our pilgrimage of faith, it is a faith pilgrimage into servanthood. It is a new way of relating. It is not power politics. It is not jockeying for position, and it is not trying to be elected. It is a new way of relating. The irony of all of this, counter-intuitively, is that only then does the grace of God emerge unbidden. It is not at our beck and call. It is not ours to master. It is not in the things we do well. Keats, in a secular mode, called this "negative capability," emptying oneself and taking the form of a servant. This goes against the grain of human nature and yet it is that for which humans were created. This pilgrimage that we are all on, faculty and students alike, is nothing less than a new means of relating to God and each other in a community called Candler. It is a pilgrimage we all make. We make it fitfully, piecemeal, backsliding, but it is our pilgrimage.

The founder of Methodism, John Wesley, spoke of going on to perfection. In the early days of Methodism the question was in fact asked of each minister, "Are you going on to perfection?" What I think Wesley had in mind was not so much being made perfect in love (at least not in an abstract sense) but rather, "Are you on a faith pilgrimage of servanthood?" Servanthood, you see, is really a sturdy form of love. Love has so many aspects, so many dimensions, and so many ways of being misunderstood. When we talk of servanthood, it means working to get rid of that exquisite "self-referentiality" to which we are all addicted. Servanthood means trying to live in a new mode, but never without other help from above.

I first saw this in a faculty member when I was in theology school years ago. His name was Richard Niebuhr, a very distinguished theologian. Of course, because of his name, students flocked to his classes. He began every class with a brief prayer. At first, I thought it was just a formality: "This is what Richard Niebuhr does; it is a good way of getting them all quiet." Then I thought, "Well maybe it is piety." Then I realized it was not that at all. His prayer was a prologue to his lecture, and he was placing it in the context of being a servant of God. It was very clear that his lectures were reflections on a very thoughtful pilgrimage. His prayers appropriately began those lectures. And, he wanted us to be participants in that servanthood.

That was my first introduction to someone who had such authority, humbling himself in public in a very authentic and genuine way. He wrote his brief, four to five line prayers, on a little note pad. One of my prize possessions is a copy of one of his prayers. We have it framed. Interestingly, his prayers so often spoke about how to escape the toils of self-regard and self-referentiality. One of his most famous books, *The Responsible Self*, was one of the results of such prayerful reflection.

A few years after theology school, Berta and I went as missionaries to Korea. I had been there in the army twelve years before. It was still war-ravaged and under great deprivation, not the Korea we know today. We were to work with university students and a cadre of colleagues. We were young and had energy and commitment and education and were idealistic and we wanted to serve nobly. I wanted to be really committed, to do something more than the conventional. I took my family halfway around the world in order to do so.

When we arrived in Korea, we were put in a remote house that hadn't been lived in for years, without a telephone. It was on rutted dirt roads and hard to get to. We found that even though we'd had a year of intensive language study, nobody understood what we were saying. You can't imagine how humiliating that is. I remembered my wife's grandmother saying in a sprightly manner, "Jimmy, don't worry. If God could make Balaam's ass speak, he can teach you Korean." I found that of little consolation. In rapid succession we had a fire; everything we shipped over by boat, everything, was robbed the first night of its arrival. Our oldest child almost died from a misdiagnosed case of scarlet fever. Berta, after having our daughter Mary, got the shingles. This cascade of events was primarily borne by the family, not by me.

We had arrived as confident Americans. Oh, we were dedicated, and we thought we knew what we were doing and we wanted to serve. We wanted to serve, but we were not really prepared to be servants. Do you understand the difference? We wanted to serve, but we wanted to serve on *our* terms, and we had all those terms taken away. We were divested of security. We were emotionally and physically depleted. We were no longer heroic.

It was at that moment that God's grace intervened in the form of our dear Christian friends in Korea. They saw us now no longer as the set-apart Americans or the privileged Americans or the confident Americans. They now saw us as not one *of* them but one *with* them. That made all the difference! No, we hadn't really emptied ourselves (most of this was involuntary), but we were emptied.

Through this experience in Korea, I saw the power that Jesus manifested and about which Paul spoke: the power of servanthood. It is always, of course, a *pilgrimage* of faith. It means being *on the road* to servanthood. And, it occurs to me how much that is needed in the church today. We have glimpses of that life, of what it can mean from time to time, and we know it is valid. That is why we are here. We are provided with a new vision. In my mind, it is a vision that has two very primary implications.

The first implication is that we are to include and not exclude. Servants do not keep people out. Servants do not choose whom they will serve. As servants, we do not demonize or curse—we bless. As disciples of Jesus we do not demonize, we include. "But they're evil!" we sometimes say. No, they are not evil. More often than not, according to Jesus, it is our self-righteousness that is evil!

The second implication of this new vision is that we reconcile. We do not avenge and we do not get even. We reconcile. We realize that dogma and position have to give way to our being servants to avoid the moral squint that so discolors our view. We learn to refuse to be led by settled opinions about world power.

To include and to reconcile as a servant on our way, as a servant-church on its way, is at the heart of our vocation. It is almost beyond belief that a bitter division has arisen over the use of the term "the reconciling church." When is the church *not* supposed to be reconciling? Are we not to be reconciling with all people? "God so loved the world." Is there a qualification on that? Granted, our pilgrimage of faith and servanthood open up many new vistas that are difficult to expand and go into, but they have the imperative, the mandate of the power of God in Christ. And, this mandate is clearly larger than the canvas of the church or the individual or even the nation. It also extends to power politics. Because of our experience in Korea and our friends there, we saw people differently, and we couldn't make empty snap judgments, characterizations of dismissal such as "the axis of evil."

This is a pilgrimage, a journey. The faculty get to share it with the students and we all take it. It is a journey into servanthood. To acknowledge that it is a difficult journey goes without saying. But, an inclusive, reconciling community of servanthood is one that the world awaits and needs, one for which the world is crying out.

Called to the Margins:
The *Missio Dei* and Faithful Christian Ministry

Kenneth L. Carder

The church in the United States confronts multiple theological, socio-logical, institutional, and cultural challenges. The statistical decline of membership in mainline denominations signals a shift in the religious landscape of the American society. For centuries Western culture and Christendom have existed as integral components of the same reality. But evidence abounds that the Constantinian era is coming to an end. Christianity is now one option among many in the marketplace of world-views, and the church is no longer viewed as a privileged institution in democratic societies. The marginalization of Christianity and the church is most evident in Europe. Yet in the United States, the signs of dimin-ished influence and cultural disestablishment of the Christian church are becoming increasingly evident, resulting in a growing sense of crisis among church leaders. Churches bemoan the loss of denominational identity and loyalty and scramble to stop the membership hemorrhage and financial shortfall. Some leaders and groups have turned to political action as the primary means of maintaining and restoring American as "a Christian nation." Church growth strategies and marketing techniques have moved to the center of the church's life, and a survival mentality dominates the mood of many judicatories, local churches, and pastors. Techniques and tactics for institutional success have replaced sharing in God's salvation of the cosmos as primary preoccupations of the church and its leaders.

The market and its accompanying consumerism have won the day as the prevailing god of American culture, including the church. The logic of exchange provides the lens through which we view the world, and consuming has become the prevailing ritual practice by which we are formed. Worth, whether it is of persons or objects or ideas, is determined by the exchange value in the marketplace. The Christian logic of grace, which ascribes worth to gift and the intrinsic value of God's creation, has been marginalized among the multiple options in the consumerist search for self-actualization and fulfillment. Religion has become another commodity, and ministry is viewed as a service to be purchased by those who have financial resources to do so. Religious symbols, stories, and rituals have been severed from their roots, thereby rendering them powerless to change persons and influence culture. They have become commodities to be used and discarded according to their utility.[1]

Disestablishment and market consumerism radically impact the church's self-understanding and the role of ministry. Disestablishment and institutional decline have motivated concern for recovery of influence and institutional renewal. The market consumerist ideology has become the popular means for addressing the "crisis" of membership loss and cultural marginalization. Faithful ministry is defined by the measures of the corporate world of growth and statistical success, and tools of the marketplace are marshaled in support of restoring the church's cultural prominence. According to this consumerist model, effective church leadership, therefore, involves mastery of the techniques and tactics of the business world. Strategic planning, systems thinking, and marketing methods become foundational rather than merely instrumental components of church leadership.

What is faithful Christian ministry in American culture of the twenty-first century? Where does ministry originate? What is the *telos* of Christian ministry? Where does it take place? What sustains Christian ministry in a culture where the church is marginalized? These are critical questions that merit serious theological and ecclesiological reflection.

Christian ministry originates in the nature and mission of God, and questions about the shape and form of ministry are fundamentally theological questions. In what follows, I want to show how the nature and mission of God challenge, *fundamentally*, a consumerist, market-driven model of the church and ministry.

---

1. For a cogent and definitive treatment of the impact on the church of consumerism, see Vincent J. Miller, *Consuming Religion: The Commodification of Culture* (New York: Continuum, 2003).

Christian Ministry Originates in the Triune God

I once asked a prominent theologian what he considered to be the primary role of a bishop. He responded that the principal role of the bishop is to hold the church and its leaders to theological discipline and integrity. He added that from his observation the church today is atheist. It affirms the existence of God but behaves as though God does not exist. The church really does not need God to be a "successful" institution, he opined; it only needs a strategic plan and a clever marketing strategy.

Here is a fundamental affirmation about Christian ministry: ministry is about God, a particular God, we call Trinity. Practicing ministry in a culture dominated by consumerism requires clarity about what seems self-evident. But in an economically driven and consumerist culture, God is another commodity available according to the self-identified needs of autonomous consumers of piety. People shop for gods and churches the same way they shop for other commodities, and the ultimate test of the reality of the gods is their ability to meet consumers' self-defined expectations. Or, in an "ecclesiocracy without ecclesiology,"[2] god is a vague presumption, and a presumed god is inevitably co-opted by the explicit gods of the prevailing culture. The Triune God, however, refuses to be supplanted or subordinated to any lesser gods, including the market, or what the Bible calls mammon!

Christian ministry begins, continues, and ends in a narrative with a different *telos* and logic than that of market consumerism. It is the story of a particular God. This God is revealed in two primal formative actions and stories from which Christian theology and practice emanate—the Exodus and the birth, death, and resurrection of Jesus Christ. Christian ministry is incorporation into, proclamation of, and participation in *the story* of God's mighty acts of deliverance, God's new creation brought near in the life, teaching, death, and resurrection of Jesus Christ, and God's continuing presence and power through the Holy Spirit working within community to bring to completion God's new creation inaugurated in Jesus Christ.

The practice of Christian ministry in a consumerist culture requires, then, that we be explicit about the God who calls, shapes, forms, and

---

2. I am indebted to C. C. Goen for this characterization of the contemporary in an article entitled "Ecclesiocracy without Ecclesiology," *American Baptist Quarterly* 10 (1991) 266–79.

empowers the Church. This is a God who delivered our forbears from the slave economy of Pharaoh, the God whose very nature and mission were revealed to Moses: "I have observed the misery of my people who are in Egypt; I have heard their cry on account of their taskmasters. Indeed, I know their sufferings, and I have come to deliver them and to bring them up out of that land to a good and broad land..." (Exod 3:7–8). This God is distinguishable from other gods in that this God defends the orphans, the widows, the sojourners—those left out of the prevailing economies, those on the margins of the dominant society. This God leads the marginalized and oppressed through the desert, replacing Pharaoh's slave economy of scarcity reserved for the privileged with a manna economy of abundance available to all.

This God became flesh in Jesus Christ, who embodies God's presence, mission, and power. This God comes among us as a vulnerable baby, was born among the marginalized of an unmarried peasant teenager in a cattle stall among those made homeless by the economic policies of Caesar, spent his early years as an immigrant in Egypt, and grew up in a working class family. He went along the lakeside announcing, "The time is fulfilled, the kingdom of God has come near; repent and believe the good news." He announced his mission in the words of Isaiah, "The Spirit of the Lord is upon me because he has anointed me to bring good news to the poor, release to the captives, recovery of sight to the blind, and to announce the year of jubilee," God's jubilee economy (Luke 4:18–19). He welcomed the vulnerable and the outcasts, healed the sick, forgave the alienated, fed the hungry, spoke truth to religious and political power. And he so closely identifies with the vulnerable and powerless—the sick, the imprisoned, the poor—that what is done to them is done to him. He was executed as a criminal and he died with forgiveness on his lips. In the resurrection, God delivered an everlasting and cosmic "yes!" to everything Jesus said and did. And God established Jesus as the firstborn of a New Creation and won the decisive victory over the principalities and powers that threaten God's reign of compassion, justice, generosity, and joy.

Central in the message of the Synoptic Gospels is the proclamation of "the kingdom of God." In Mark's Gospel, Jesus launches his ministry with this announcement, "The time is fulfilled, and the kingdom of God has come near; repent, and believe the good news" (Mark 1:15). Jesus is the incarnation of the reign of God, the firstborn of the new age that is dawning. As a sign, foretaste, and instrument of the kingdom of God, Jesus intentionally went to the margins of first century Palestine and incorporated the poor, the lame, the vulnerable, the powerless and declared that it is among these that the kingdom exists. He repeatedly challenged the popular images of success and power, and he welcomed the least and despised into the center of God's activity and presence.

As Gene Davenport has consistently reminded us, a basic presupposition of the New Testament writers is the division of the history of creation into two *aeons*, or two ages.[3] In the old *aeon*, the creation is dominated by principalities and powers—structures and practices that counter God's intention and thwart the thriving of creation and human existence. The old world is characterized by exploitation, alienation, violence, hostility and death. The new *aeon*, or new age of God's reign, is dominated by God's love, righteousness, justice, and shalom. For the New Testament, the new age of God's reign is inaugurated in the life, teachings, death, and resurrection of Jesus. As the old world is characterized by sin and death, the new world of God's reign is marked by the restoration of God's purposes and the renewal of the whole creation. As the Apostle Paul affirmed, "He [Christ] is the image of the invisible God, the firstborn of all creation . . . and through him God was pleased to reconcile to himself all things, whether on earth or in heaven, by making peace through the blood of the cross" (Col 1:15–20). In 2 Corinthians, the Apostle declared, "So if anyone is in Christ, there is a new creation: everything old has passed away; see everything has become new!" (2 Cor 5:17).

God's mission, the *missio Dei*, is the transformation of the whole creation in accordance with the new creation inaugurated in Jesus Christ; and the church is called into being as a herald, sign, and instrument of the new creation. The church, therefore, lives and serves at the intersection of the old and the new, or as Davenport calls it "the overlapping of the ages." The church, then, exists on the margins (or edges) of the world dominated by sin and death and the new creation characterized by God's reign of compassion, justice, righteousness, and peace.

Central to the nature and mission of the Triune God is preferential concern for and presence with those the Hebrew Scriptures call "the

---

3. This is a recurring theme in Gene Davenport's writing, teaching, and preaching. See *King Jesus: Servant, Lord, Soul Brother* (Nashville: Graded, 1972); *Into the Darkness: Discipleship in the Sermon on the Mount* (Nashville: Abingdon, 1988); *Powers and Principalities* (Cleveland: Pilgrim, 2003).

orphans, the widows, and the sojourners (the immigrants)." From the Hebrew Prophets to the ministry of Jesus, justice and compassion for those on the margins of society—the poor, the oppressed, the vulnerable and powerless—is the decisive and determinative mark of faithfulness to the Triune God. God dwells among the marginalized and is ever working to transform the structures and practices of the creation in accordance with the reign of justice, compassion, generosity, and peace.

This is the theological framework and grounding for the church's existence and for all Christian ministry.

The Church as Marginalized Community

While many see the loss of cultural prominence as a threat to the church, it may be an occasion for reclaiming theological and missional identity. Charles Bayer sees the demise of Christendom as an opportunity for "discover[ing] and liv[ing] into a new ecclesial paradigm."[4] "In this paradigm," Bayer says, "the church interprets its cultural and religious marginalization as providential in that it re-turns the church to the generative site for its mission and ministry: the margins, with and on behalf of the marginalized."[5] Hendrick Pieterse adds that by turning toward the margins, the church "can grasp for our day the simple but profound truth . . . the church's healing into faithfulness lies in the company of those despised, marginalized, and excluded. . . ."[6]

The margins are the appropriate location of the church; and the disestablishment of the church in American society is an opportunity to reclaim an ecclesial identity as a marginalized community in service to the *missio Dei*. As a people bearing the *imago Dei*, the church is only the church when it owns its identity as an alternative community and joins God on the margins. It is from the margins that the church bears witness to the God of the Exodus and Jesus; and it is among the vulnerable, the

---

4. Quoted by Hendrick R. Pieterse in a paper delivered at the 2007 Oxford Institute for Theological Studies and published by the General Board of Higher Education and Ministry in a monogram entitled, "Opting for the Margins, Again: Why United Methodists Need the Poor to be the Church." The quote is from Charles H. Bayer, *A Resurrected Church: Christianity after the Death of Christendom* (St. Louis: Chalice, 2001) 2.

5. Ibid.

6. Ibid., 3.

oppressed, the poor, the imprisoned, the sick, the pushed aside that the church is a visible sign, foretaste, and instrument of God's new creation.

As an alternative community within the larger society, the church itself is in its life and practice a marginalized people.[7] Claiming our identity as a community on the margins of the old world and God's reign in Jesus Christ and joining God's presence among those on the margins of society are more faithful responses to disestablishment than being so incorporated in society that the church has no distinctive qualities apart from the broader culture. Only by claiming identity and mission on the margins can the church be an agent of reconciliation and transformation of culture; and the challenge confronting those who are called to lead the church is to claim the church's identity as a marginalized community and to engage the people who live on the margins of American society—the poor, the imprisoned, the immigrants, the abused, and the vulnerable.

Toward Reclaiming Ministry on the Margins

What will it take for the church to reclaim its identity and ministry on the margins, and how do we call forth, form, deploy, and sustain pastors who are motivated and equipped to lead the church toward the margins? It will not be the result of strategic planning processes designed by systems theorists to preserve or recover cultural dominance or enhance institutional success. Such methods and approaches only exacerbate captivity to the old age dominated by principalities and powers that maintain the current status of the marginalized, while preserving the privileges of those already advantaged by the prevailing systems. Opting for the consumerist market ideology and methods as the means of countering disestablishment of the church is to substitute acquiescence to the prevailing culture for being an agent of transformation of the culture.

Reclaiming ministry on the margins requires nothing less than conversion, turning away from the powers of the old age and reorienting toward the new reality wrought in Jesus Christ. The invitation is the same as the one issued by Jesus along the Galilean lake, "The kingdom of God

---

7. Stanley Hauerwas has been at the forefront of interpreting the church's mission in terms of its identity as an alternative community. Earlier popular books by Hauerwas and William Willimon put the image clearly on the theological and ecclesial agenda. See *Resident Aliens: Life in the Christian Colony* (Nashville: Abingdon, 1989) and *Where Resident Aliens Live: Exercises for Christian Practice* (Nashville: Abingdon, 1996).

has come near, repent and believe the good news" (Mark 1:15). The first step is to hear the call to the margins as "good news" from the One who lives among those on the margins and who invites us to share in God's grace, which is the presence and power of God to create, forgive, heal, reconcile, and transform.

Hearing the call, however, requires that we first acknowledge the current social location of the mainline church in the United States. The mainline churches in general, and the United Methodist Church in particular, are part of the prevailing middle-class culture, economically situated to participate in the consumerist culture by choosing where to live, where and how often to travel, with access to medical care and adequate food, education, shelter, and clothing. But social class is more than a matter of economics. Class influences our tastes in music and art, our speech and communication patterns, the way we make decisions as individuals and groups, styles of worship, and our perspectives on issues.[8] We see in accordance with where we stand, and the mainline church in the United States sees through the lens of middle-class privilege. All locations have blind spots, and affluence tends to blind us to the gifts of those without affluence.

The church, therefore, needs those on the margins in order to see clearly its failures and opportunities, and to claim its identity as a community on the margins. Our middle-class location, however, separates us from those on the margins. Consequently, the church must intentionally seek out the marginalized, form friendships, and enter into community with them in living the new creation brought near in Jesus Christ. Rather than forging relationships by paternalistic charity, relationships are to be formed in the mutuality of shared grace and common commitment to God's reign of compassion, justice, generosity, and peace.

Turning toward the margins will require a renewed emphasis on teaching and theological reflection at all levels of church leadership. Since Christian stories, symbols, and liturgies have become commodities, and thereby have been severed from their historical and theological roots, catechesis is essential for the recovery of the transformative power of the stories, symbols, and liturgies. Biblical scholarship and academic theology have made available enormous resources for probing the depth of the

8. For an insightful description of class and its impact on the church, see Tex Sample's *Blue Collar Resistance and the Politics of Jesus: Doing Ministry with Working Class Whites* (Nashville: Abingdon, 2007).

story of God's salvation and its implications for living as a marginalized community among marginalized people. The church's failure to teach has contributed to the church's amnesia, its captivity to consumerist culture, and its lost identity as people created in the *imago Dei* who share in *missio Dei*.

Gene Davenport's life and ministry demonstrate the importance and consequence of faithful teaching that leads the church to the margins. A distinguishing mark of the pastors I have known who were influenced by Gene is a deep understanding of God as having a preferential relationship with "the orphans, the widows, and the sojourners." They "get" the concept of the two *aeons*, and they form communities and congregations that live now in the light of the present and coming reign of God's compassion, justice, generosity, and peace. As the bishop of several of Gene's former students, I can testify to their commitment to the gospel logic of grace that challenges the market logic of exchange. They opt for ministry on the margins rather than pursuing the consumerist signs of success and security. They teach what they have been taught: the gospel!

Catechesis, however, is more than the imparting of information about the stories of God's salvation acts and God's identification with "the least of these." Learning about Scripture, church history, Christian doctrines, and ethical precepts is only part of the role of catechesis. Forming persons and communities in accordance with scripture, tradition, doctrine, and ethics is fundamental to Christian catechesis. Otherwise, the Christian faith is another form of Gnosticism, whereby we are saved by special knowledge unrelated to everyday life.

Therefore, practices and disciplines that form individuals and communities into the *imago Dei* are essential components of the teaching ministry. Practicing "the means of grace" has been integral to Christian life and ministry—prayer, reading the Scriptures, theological reflection, private and public worship, the sacraments, and what John Wesley called "conference" or Christian conversation.

The most neglected discipline or practice, however, is friendship with the poor, the imprisoned, the sick, the vulnerable. Yet the Bible says far more about visitation of the poor than it says about prayer, and Jesus made relationships with "the least of these" the criteria by which the church will be judged (Matt 25:31–46). We cannot really *know God* in the biblical sense apart from relationships with the people who live on the margins—the poor, the imprisoned, the abused, the powerless, the pushed aside.

Catechesis that includes engagement on the margins requires intentionality and creativity on the part of all those who teach the Christian faith, from college and seminary professors to pastors and church schoolteachers and parents. Personal relationships with people of the margins are as essential for Christian formation as reading sacred texts. Extensive immersion experiences on the margins should be required of all seeking ordination or certification as leaders in the church; and, engagement with the marginalized in the community should be part of the criteria by which the faithfulness of a congregation and its leaders are evaluated. How nearly the congregation resembles the ministry of Jesus and the new age of God's reign must become the primary measures of its success, not its membership and attendance statistics.

Moving to the margins requires the form of servant leadership embodied in Jesus Christ and described in this early Christian hymn:

> Let this same mind be in you that was in Christ Jesus,
>> who, though he was in the form of God,
>> did not regard equality with God as something to be exploited,
> but emptied himself,
>> taking the form of a servant,
>> being born in human likeness.
> And being found in human form,
>> he humbled himself
>> and became obedient to the point of death—
>> even death on a cross.
> Therefore God also highly exalted him
>> and gave him the name,
> that is above every name,
>> so that at the name of Jesus,
>> every knee should bend,
> in heaven and on earth and under the earth,
>> and every tongue should confess
>> that Jesus Christ is Lord,
> to the glory of God the Father (Phil 2:5–11).

Conclusion

The church has always confronted challenges to its identity and mission. Sometimes the challenge has come in the form of open resistance and persecution by the dominant culture. Cultural accommodation, however, has represented the most formidable test of the church's faithfulness to its nature and calling. When the church takes on the qualities of the dominant culture and defines its success or faithfulness by the support it receives from the culture, the church ignores the people on the margins or views them as objects of occasional charity. Rather than solidarity with "the orphans, the widows, and the sojourners," the church cultivates solidarity with the powerful, the privileged, and the advantaged.

The cultural disestablishment and institutional decline of the church in North America may be God's gift and call to "remember the rock from which [we] were hewn, the quarry from which [we] were dug" (Isa 51:1). The church originated on the margins, and it exists at the intersection of the world as it is and the world God intends, on the margins between the reign of God already present and the reign of God yet to come. Claiming our identity as a marginal community and intentionally pitching our tent among the marginalized of the earth may be the means by which the God of the Exodus and Jesus brings renewal to the American church.

Renewal, however, comes as a gift from God in God's own time. Faithful ministry involves trusting who Jesus is, doing what Jesus commands, going where Jesus goes, welcoming those for whom Jesus died, and anticipating the final triumph of "the firstborn of the new creation." Jesus comes among the marginalized, identifies with "the least of these," calls disciples to a life of service with the poor and oppressed, lives and dies among the pushed aside and the vulnerable, welcomes the outcasts and despised into a new community, and triumphs over all that would thwart God's reign of justice, compassion, generosity, and peace. We, therefore, can move to the margins with confidence and hope. Gene Davenport has modeled such faithful ministry.

The Babylonian Captivity of the Church—
The American Edition

M. Douglas Meeks

In his at once tightly argued and richly poetic book *Into the Darkness: Discipleship in the Sermon on the Mount,* Gene Davenport displays in stark terms the captivity of the church in our society.[1] But it is also a book filled with hope for freedom in Jesus Christ. "For freedom Christ has set you free. Therefore do not submit again to a yoke of slavery." This has been a keynote of Gene Davenport's scholarly career driven by a passion for the freedom of the church under the gospel. The fruit can be seen in two generations of students who struggle against the forces that assault the church, from within and without, and make it captive.

The Protestant Reformation began with Luther's condemnation of the church that had enslaved itself to the forces of darkness. Luther sought the faithfulness of the church during the historical transition from a feudal economy to the nascent forms of a market economy. But we must put the matter in the present tense, for, with Davenport, our concern has to be the captivity of the American mainstream churches. Though some aspects of our context are, of course, vastly different from Luther's, the terms of the church's enslavement in our time are recognizable in Luther's manifesto. In *The Babylonian Captivity of the Church* (1520) Luther condemns the "Papacy [as] the Kingdom of Babylon and the power of Nimrod, the mighty hunter."[2] The papal system's identification with empire had led to distortions of the church by the misuse of power and the delusions of greed. The church's lordly splendor masked its pitiful captivity. Its captivity made it impotent to follow its Lord. Under the lordship

---

1. Davenport, *Into the Darkness: Discipleship in the Sermon on the Mount* (Nashville: Abingdon, 1988) 20.

2. In Luther's *Works,* vol. 36, *Word and Sacrament* (Philadelphia: Fortress, 1959).

of Jesus Christ, argues Luther, there can be no lords or systems of lordship in the church. Yet behind Luther's deadly attack on the profoundly misshapen governance of the church lies a sophisticated critique of the importation of an economy that blasphemes the "economy of God." The church had made itself captive by the misuse of the gifts given it by its Lord. It had shirked its responsibility to God's own economy of grace. This is what makes Luther's piece sear our conscience in our time.

In the sixteenth century, the selling of indulgences was a neat ecclesiastical development scheme to fill the coffers of the church. The church needs money to survive and expand, argued the leaders of the Roman Church, and in sixteenth-century central and southern Europe, money is increasingly not just a means of exchange; it is also a commodity to be bought and sold. Why should the church not enter into the financial systems that are becoming the index of power? Why should the church not profit by the coin of the realm? In so doing, according to Luther, the church has made a market where there could be no market. The genius of following a clearly profitable economy has enthralled the church to a system of lordship that denies its Lord. To preserve itself the church depends on polity instead of the promises and commands of the gospel.

The Present Situation of Mainstream Churches

The situation is familiar in our context, where the temptation for mainstream churches that are losing hold on numbers and money is to follow any method that would keep the church afloat. The captivity of our churches is due in no small measure to our delusions about economy, not just this or that economics, not just free-market or socialist economics, but delusions about the fundamental meaning of the ancient term "economy" as the human means of bringing human beings together for surviving and thriving. That is, despite all of the ways modern economics, especially neoclassical economics, camouflages its reality, *economy* is about surviving (*survivre*, living through the day) and the human relations that make for the surviving of all. Neoclassical economics overlooks two essential aspects of economy in the scriptures (and in much of antiquity for that matter), namely, 1) humane economy is not self-regulating but rather depends on the fabric of human relationships, and 2) economy is about livelihood. The earliest Christian movements took over this basic form of economy as household, but the gospel of these movements radically redefined the character of livelihood and the kind of relationships that are necessary to the fullness of life. Livelihood, for the church, became the new being in Jesus Christ nourished by the "bread of life" and the Spirit's transformation of human relationships so that there are no longer the crushing divisions between free and slave, man and woman, rich and poor (Gal 3:28).

The church is a kind of "political economy." It has a formal analogy to various political economies in history. But the church is called by the gospel to be radically different materially from the political economies we have known. While the church always lives in the midst of a dominant political economy, if it simply reflects the surrounding economy it is soon captive to this economy. The church jeopardizes itself as the Household (*oikos*, economy) of Jesus Christ when it does not hear and live the gospel.

So from an ecclesiological perspective, "political economy" refers first of all to the economy of God (*oikonomia tou theou*), that is, the way God is redeeming and will redeem the world as seen in the scriptural narration of Jesus and the Spirit. Secondly, it refers to the church's participation in the Triune communion of God and in God's work of redeeming the world. The worldly experience of the church receives its shape and authority from this participation.

Ecclesiology should, however, take account of the formal similarities to political economy which in almost all historical instances displays these four aspects:

1. work or production,
2. distribution or inclusive property, the right of access to what it takes to live and flourish,
3. the relation (often reciprocal) of those in the household, and
4. the natural environment from which the community lives.

In the Household of Jesus Christ, the way these four aspects of political economy are treated decides the shape of the church. In the power of the Holy Spirit, the church seeks a *graced work* that serves God's answer to the prayer Christians pray on behalf of all human beings, "Give us this day our daily bread." The church seeks to distribute what is necessary for life according to the *logic of grace* instead of the logic of pricing so that all can be included in livelihood. It is an economy that begins with the assumption of abundance, not scarcity. The church lives by the God-given new being by which those in the household live according to *God's gifts of giving, forgiving, and hospitality*. And, finally, the church embraces God's gift of *creation*, not as the stuff of production and profit, but as our home, as our opportunity for life only if we recognize nature's irreducible right to flourish. So the church is a political economy in radically differ-ent ways. Owning these different ways in our time is the way we work out what it means for the church to be "in the world but not of it."

If the church is in an attenuated sense a *political* economy, it must constantly ask, as it does every time it worships, from which power does the church receive its authority?[3] Which power is the church to serve? If the church does not know and experience the power from which it lives, how can it stand up against false power? Though we normally think of Luther's hermeneutic in terms of "justification by grace through faith" and "law and gospel," perhaps his most important hermeneutical key was expressed in the *Heidelberg Disputation* (1519), in which he developed Paul's central claim that the power of God is the cross of Christ (1 Cor 1). Thinking of the church as a political economy in the power of the cross does indeed, as the *Heidelberg Disputation* frightfully demonstrates, turn church and world on their heads. It makes the church transparent. It brings the church into the light, no longer allowing its masking by ceremony and ritual that *appear* to be gospel-formed, but instead have become signs for an inhuman political economy in captivity.

Does the church today jeopardize its gospel freedom by seeking to solve its problems of decline by the market logic? Have the dictates of the global market economy taken the place of the cross of the resurrected one as the sole power for life? Does the church, too, seek future, security, and life in the logic of the exchange of commodities and the accumula-tion of wealth? Is the church captive to an economic system that makes God's grace a commodity? In his time, Luther gave a clear answer of "yes" to these questions. The church, he claimed, had made itself captive by turning Word and Sacrament into commodities and thereby ruining the economy of grace. The church exchanged the truth for a lie by placing the means of God's grace, Word and Sacrament, into the exchange of com-modities. It thereby pretended to control salvation.

To Luther's concentration on the cross of Christ we should add today a focus on those who must stand in the shadow of the cross: the poor.

---

3. See Bernd Wannenwetsch, *Political Worship: Ethics for Christian Citizens*, trans. Margaret Kohl (Oxford: Oxford University Press, 2004).

The Church and the Poor

If the church must include, according to the gospel, the presence of the poor, it must be a political economy that is genuinely alternative to market exchange. For a long time theological attempts to address economy could be countered by the simple, uncontested claim that there is no economy except that described by modern economic orthodoxy. This leaves theology in a tight place, since neither the church nor the poor can appear in the neoclassical economic theory. If ecclesial, social, and political policies are governed by this theory, the church and the poor are, quite simply, publicly occluded.

Both ecclesiology and the church's relation to the world have to be rethought in relation to the poor. In fact, mainstream North Atlantic churches will discover a more faithful ecclesiology in face of their collapsing ecclesial structures precisely in practiced, instituted conformity with the Triune God's life with the poor. Something similar can be said about society's general perception of political economy. It will find its way out of captivity to the illusion of the self-regulating market through incorporating the poor in the public household.

We should be guided by these convictions: the church has its own distinctive economy largely composed of "noneconomic economies." The public economy must include economies that incorporate the poor. The church's contribution to the state and the political economy of our time is making clear the necessity of noneconomic economies for the transformation of market economy and the inclusion of the poor in the public institutions of the political economy, and, indeed, the necessity of noneconomic economies for the successful practice of any public economy.

We turn now, as did Luther, to Word and Sacrament as keys to the preeminent noneconomic economy of the church. The logic of the gospel and the life-forming action of the sacraments are yet today the way of freedom from the church's captivity.

Word as Gospel

Without the preaching and hearing of the gospel, the church does not know which power to serve according to which means. The fragility of the church has nothing to do with its strength as determined by the calculus of the market, for when it seems strong and affluent, it is likely in most danger of losing its freedom and its soul. Today the church's living as the economy of God depends, in the first place, on discerning the difference between commodity exchange and *charis* (gift or grace).

The market system depends on the logic of exchange, *quid pro quo.* Excluding the right to own slaves or physically to coerce others, and recognizing the merely intermittent success of persuading others to barter, the remaining possibility to meet my need is a contingent offer of a benefit to others in exchange for their fulfilling my need.[4] Money as such a universal benefit makes the exchange relationship universally available.[5] No one can doubt the great benefit of exchange relationships in allocating goods and services. But modern market anthropology tends toward the exclusion of gift in the picture of the human being, harboring the ancient prejudices against gifting and dreaming up additional ones. Market human beings are suspicious of gifting because it entails ambiguity fed by the faint sense of debt and domination.

The response of the Christian view of the human being to artificial scarcity, debt, and commodity exchange is grace. A Christian anthropology focused on gift giving as grace, rather than on commodity exchange, points to the triune community's freeing of human giving from the reality of debt.

This is apparent, first, in the way God gives in creating. God gives without the guarantee of return.[6] This is so because God gives everything

4. Charles E. Lindblom, *The Market System* (New Haven: Yale University Press, 2001) 53–54. Hegel described the modern society as a "system of needs" in which we relate to each other by making offers to meet each other's needs by an exchange of benefits. *Hegel's Philosophy of Right*, trans. T. M. Knox (Oxford: Clarendon, 1952) 126–28.

5. Karl Polanyi, *The Great Transformation* (Boston: Beacon, 1957). As Lindblom observes, both barter and money economies are taken to be great advances over gift economies, because "gifts obligate the recipient to make a reciprocal gift. Since the receiver decides how and when to reciprocate and can delay," reciprocal gift giving "offers little opportunity to obtain a specified benefit by my offer of benefits." Lindblom further notes, "Some object of value that everyone is pleased to have enters into exchanges. Whether seashells, gold, or paper certificates, it is *money.* With money, the need for coincidence drops from two to only one—the second coincidence is no longer necessary. Although you still have to find someone who can offer you what you want, you do not now have to find one who wants a particular service or object that you can offer, for you offer not a particular service or object but the universally desired object. *To induce a carpenter or metalworker to help with your house, you do not have to find those who want your performance or objects. Any carpenter or hardware supplier will accept money as a sufficient inducement to give you the help you want.*" Lindblom, *Market System*, 54–55 (italics in original).

6. For the following, cf. Kathryn Tanner, *Jesus, Humanity and the Trinity: A Brief Systematic Theology.* (Minneapolis: Fortress Press, 2001), 82–95.

that we are, and thus there is nothing in us that could establish an obligation toward God. "What do you have that you did not receive? And if you received it, why do you boast as if it were not a gift?" (1 Cor 4:7). Furthermore, God gives us Christ, and in him union with the Triune Community and in this all things (Rom 8:32), simply because of our need, not because we are deserving. God's *pleroma* lacks nothing we could pay back. We have nothing more to return than what God has already given us. God's gifts to us are not loans, nor does God stop giving when we squander or misuse God's gifts. Even when we fail to give, God is willing to give more. Our failure to give, to be sure, removes the blessing of giving that God intends for us, but it does not cause God's giving to cease. Everything about our lives should be a reflection of this gift.

The logic of grace means that salvation cannot be priced. The self-giving of God in the cross of Christ precludes a scale of payment in God's relation with human beings. The "logic" of grace is the gifting of Jesus Christ who is both gift and giver of gift. Grace is not a commodity to be exchanged. Salvation cannot be earned or purchased. The *quid pro quo* relationship is a false reading of the gospel to enhance one's position of power; it prevents the church from participating in the *oikonomia tou theou*. From the perspective of grace, religion is not a "commerce with the gods" that enslaves through guilt and fear of death. We cannot bribe, barter with, repay, extort, assuage, or sacrifice our way to God. We are not in competition with God and therefore cannot negotiate with God.

Neither does the gift of the cross produce an infinite debt that is in principle unpayable. It is not that in the cross God has somehow recompensed our debts or tendered the obedience we could not render. Rather, God cancels the possibility of debt itself and, therefore, debt economy as the source of obligation and security.[7] But, according to Paul, the decisive point is that in giving us an unreturnable gift, God forgives our debt. If God accounts us as having no debt, the possibility of our being restored to God's economy of graceful giving is opened up. In this sense, God's redeeming work transforms the economy of debt into the economy of

---

7. "We are ransomed on the cross from the suffering and oppression in which a debt economy has thrown us; taken from the cross we are returned to our original owner God, to God's kingdom of unconditional giving, snatched out of the world of deprivation and injustice from which we suffer because of our poverty, our inability to pay what others demand of us." Tanner, *Jesus, Humanity and the Trinity*, 88.

grace. The appropriate prayer to be prayed in the economy of grace is, "Forgive us our debts as we forgive our debtors." To be the *homo economicus* in God's economy of grace means that we are shaped by God's giving rather than by maximizing utility.

If God gives to the creation in a way that undermines debt economy, we are left with the question *how* we should give. God's excessive giving creates space and time for human reciprocity. "Owe no one anything but love." Our obedience in giving is not a matter of clearing our debt to God, and yet God does give to us with the expectation that God's giving will be reflected in our covenanted giving.

Sacrament: Life at Table with Jesus Christ

The sacraments enflesh the economy of God. Luther took the sacraments completely out of the system of humanly mediated salvation that could be bought and sold. A true sacrament is a promise and a sign instituted by Jesus. While Luther deals with baptism and penance in *The Babylonian Captivity of the Church*, he concentrates on the "visible word" of the Lord's Supper. He focuses the economy of God on the meal, on the table to which all are invited. All for whom Christ died can expect to be confronted, forgiven, hoped for, and loved at the Lord's Table. Thus the meal enacts two universals of Christian theology: 1) the universal offer of salvation—Christ has died for all human beings; and 2) all have sinned and fallen short of the glory of God.

The "law of grace" is also enfleshed at the table. The bread of Jesus (blessed, broken, and given) cannot be a commodity and becomes the criterion of what is a commodity and what is not. What is necessary for the life of human beings claimed by God cannot be a commodity or at least exhaustively a commodity. The work of the congregation in its surroundings depends on this discernment. It is the Host's table manners and household rules that have to be followed in the economy of grace. Grace has a structure, a form, a shape that we know above all in the life and relationships of Jesus. Human desire finds its direction and goal, not in the luxury of the world, but in the common life of Christ's household and in this household's self-giving to the world. The Supper is to lead to Eucharistic living in the whole of life. The supper is shared bread with the friends of Jesus, the strangers, the *paraoikoi*. The real presence of Jesus makes them present. We receive God's grace as we share God's grace with the other who is excluded because the other has nothing to exchange. This meal is life-giving intimacy with the poor.

The sacraments are the noneconomic economy in the Household of Jesus Christ. We turn now to their analogues.

Household, Redistribution, and Reciprocity

Karl Polanyi viewed redistribution, reciprocity, and household as real depictions of the sources and destinations of the flow of goods.[8] They are forms of integration demonstrating how societies can be and have been organized without markets. They function without the logic of commodity exchange. In an analogous way, sacraments give signals about the origin and destinations of goods given by God and how they are to be given by the gifted. Baptism and the Lord's Supper are not the possession of the church; they are the instruments by which God the Holy Spirit creates the economy of church.

Human history, however, clearly shows that these forms of integrating economy (household, redistribution, and reciprocity) contain within them the very negative realities that led the Enlightenment's urge to freedom to endorse the market as the single means of integrating economy. Household emphasizes the *status* of persons instead of contract. Redistribution focuses on *centricity* instead of the autonomy of the individual. Reciprocity entails *generosity and gifting* with their predilection to indebtedness and patronizing control instead of the freedom of exchange leading to equilibrium. Over against the threats within these forms of integration, modern economic orthodoxy presents itself as the exclusive form of economy: self-interest within unregulated market exchange in which greed is to be controlled by the working of the "invisible hand." No external authority, no church or state, needed.

There is, then, no doubt that forms of redistribution, reciprocity, and household can and have been as brutal as the current institutions of exchange and have to be redeemed, like exchange, from the *libido dominandi* incipient in each. The humanization of these three forms of the flow of goods depends in its actuality on the human motives behind them and on the assumptions about nature, the human being, and the media of

8. See Karl Polanyi, *Trade and Market in the Early Empires: Economies in History and Theory* (Glencoe, IL: Free, 1957), and Polanyi, *The Livelihood of Man*, ed. Harry W. Pearson (New York: Academic, 1977) 19ff.

the flow of goods that drive them. Contemporary economic and political thought often simply precludes these older forms of the flow of goods as anathema to progress. But the imagination of a new ecclesiology will require thinking the *oikonomia tou theou* in relation to these forms. So will public economic institutions that do not collapse under the weight of the exclusion of the poor.

Household: The Law of Grace

The history of *oikonomia* acknowledges the fact that human beings are shaped according to the economy or household in which they live. Adam Smith and Karl Marx were not the first to make this claim; it was held by Amos and Jeremiah, Plato and Aristotle, Paul, the Church Fathers, and the whole Christian tradition until the seventeenth century. This perspective recognizes that different modes of subsistence and of acquiring property (access to livelihood) produce "different ways of life" or different associations of human beings. Human beings are constituted by their associations and by the goods their associations serve. Relations of those in the household precede and ground all other concerns of economy.

As we have seen, some form of economy has always existed insofar as human beings have lived together for survival. There are many forms of economy, many ways to put together household for survival. Household may not have been the earliest form of economy, but it is the most consistent form of economy through human history. Economy was not thematized or brought to consciousness as long as it was embedded in society. Economy as an intellectual theme appears when Aristotle discovered what happens to livelihood with the introduction of commerce and trade. Aristotle's genius is the recognition of what is lost with the coming of commerce. Before trade and commerce existed livelihood was accomplished without the conscious abstraction from the means of livelihood.

Modern society is built on *contract*, while household economies rest on *status*. Community dominates where economy is embedded in noneconomic institutions.[9] Contract is the legal aspect of exchange; a

9. For Ferdinand Toennies and many other modern social theorists community corresponded to status, and contract to society. The lives of persons are intimately "embedded in the tissue of common experience" while society is never far removed from the "cash nexus" (Thomas Carlyle). The problem was how to restore community without

society based on contract should possess an institutionally separate and motivationally distinct economic sphere of exchange, namely, the market. Status on the other hand corresponds to an earlier condition that roughly goes with reciprocity and redistribution.[10] Status derives from kinship and adoption and is generally set by birth or primary relations in community. A person's position in the family or community determines his or her rights and duties. Valuing (pricing) and access to livelihood depend on the relative standing relations in the community of partners in the exchange. Prices should conform to the rule of justice that is usually based in a shared understanding of communal goods.

The enormous problem of *oikonomia* is the hardening of status. For Aristotle the status of slaves determined what they were due. A great promise of modernity is that contract emancipates the individual from status.[11] The modern race and gender liberations, however, are always ambiguous if they merely assume that contract liberates, for contract never assures that one will be included in what it takes to survive and thrive. Rather, inclusion in a household dedicated to surviving and thriving depends on a change in one's status. And this is precisely the New Testament theme: a change of status before God and in relation to the community through God's grace: from sinner to forgiven one, from unrighteous to justified, from enemy to friend, from indebted to ransomed, from stranger (*paraoikoi*) to one at home, from privileged to accepted.[12] Without the practice of the noneconomic economy of household, the

---

returning to authority and paternalism, how to advance to a higher form of community. This was a kind of "post-society" stage, a cooperative phase of human existence retaining the advantages of technological progress and individual freedom while restoring the wholeness of life. See Polanyi, *Trade*, 70.

10. "As long as these latter forms of integration prevail, no concept of an economy need arise. The elements of the economy are here embedded in noneconomic institutions, the economic process itself being instituted through kinship, marriage, age-groups, secret societies, totemic associations, and public solemnities. The term 'Economic life' would here have no meaning." Polanyi, *Trade and Market in the Early Empires*, 70.

11. Already under Roman law status was significantly replaced by contract: rights and duties derived from bilateral agreements.

12. Many studies have shown the way in which the Jesus movement radically changed the Greco-Roman meaning of *oikos* in the experience of the household (economy) of Jesus Christ. Representative are May L. Coloe, *Dwelling in the Household of God: Johannine Ecclesiology and Spirituality* (Collegeville, MN: Liturgical, 2007); Michael R. Trainor, *The Quest for Home: The Household in Mark's Community* (Collegeville, MN: Liturgical, 2001).

church remains a mélange of individuals in pursuit of a market of needs fulfillment. Without the practice of the noneconomic economy of household the poor are permanently excluded from the community that is singularly able to address their poverty in all of its dimensions. We have become a society of contract holders, one pretended boon of which is the notion that we can solve poverty from a distance. But, poverty can only be diminished in intimacy with the poor.

If sacraments are signs of the flow of God's grace and the integration of the economy of God, then baptism is the sign of changed status, a new creation covenanted to the integrity of God's household as given by the law of grace. The church is the sign of God's redemption in history, though it points well beyond itself to God's redeeming presence in the world. Redemption looks *in micro* like the economy the church is called to be by participation the economy of the Triune God. If the church cannot embody or point to this economy, it no longer bears the signs of redemption. Everyone belongs to the economy of God in the first sense given above. Though not everyone belongs to the Household of Jesus Christ, the practice of hospitality in Jesus Christ means making home for the homeless in society. Hence, the church must hold the state responsible for giving the social value to the poor that citizenship demands. In living according to the law of grace, the church can witness that persons must be embedded in community and economy must be embedded in society and regulated by the state.

Reciprocity: Grace as Covenanted

The hatred of reciprocal giving in our society is profound. It ruins market exchange. But this hatred also undermines the noneconomic economies on which even the market is ultimately dependent. In the system in which it is assumed that everything can be priced, the economy of grace works to open up spheres resembling reciprocity that are beyond pricing and commodity exchange and therefore can be shaped by gifts which are not returnable or that are reciprocal.

An important discussion about the relative merits of gift and loan has arisen around the impressive results of micro lending in parts of the developing world.[13] But the fact that micro lending does not work

13. M. Yunus and K. Weber, *Creating a World without Poverty: Social Business and*

in the most impoverished areas of North America and in many parts of the developing world is an indication that the practices necessary for involvement in the market require communities in which many generations of communal reciprocal relations create the possibility of trust, self-confidence, cultural identity, education, and family stability. There can be no human dignity without *giving*.[14] It is generally true that "non-gifted people" cannot "successfully" enter the market or any other association for that matter.

Redistribution

Finally, the noneconomic economies of redistribution are abhorred in our public economy because they seem to require some form of centricity. Enlightenment liberative theories detest storehouses controlled by throne and altar. But the fact that the market does not distribute the means of livelihood to the poor means that the poor are excluded from livelihood. Theology's undervaluing of the doctrine of Providence[15] and its inattention to the theological reality of alms[16] are signs of its inattention to the poor and the church. The narratives of manna (Exod 16) and of redistribution in Acts 2–4 are a testimony that alms are not an expression of personal generosity (as market ideology would have it) but rather an obligation because of God's claims on the poor. Provision for the poor obligated for the church by God's law of grace and for the state by the law of humanity means the enormously difficult reintroduction on the local and global levels of the legal protection of *inclusive* property as well as exclusive property.

No one should assume that freedom from the captivity of present day churches will be easy. But by the grace we know in the Crucified Risen One, we might again learn how to practice the noneconomic economies God intends for the poor and thus for our redemption.

The Future of Capitalism (New York: Public Affairs, 2007).

14. The work of Amartya Sen is ample testimony to this. See his *Development as Freedom* (New York: Anchor, 1999).

15. Charles M. Wood, *The Question of Providence* (Louisville: Westminster John Knox, 2008).

16. Susan R. Holman, *The Hungry are Dying: Beggars and Bishops in Roman Cappadocia* (Oxford: Oxford University Press, 2001). Kelly S. Johnson, *The Fear of Beggars: Stewardship and Poverty in Christian Ethics* (Grand Rapids: Eerdmans, 2007).

Prayer—The Final Frontier *

Phyllis Tickle

Prayer is the simplest of terms in the lexicon of religion; but one must always be chary of simplicity, and especially so in matters of religion. As often as not, it hides, as is true in the case of prayer, a complexity of infinite beauty and infinite peril.

In books and chapters of books like this one, prayer is usually spoken of as a discipline or practice. Sometimes it is addressed by spheres of practice or mechanisms of delivery like private prayer, corporate prayer, liturgical prayer, and rote prayer. More commonly in the Protestant tradition, it is discussed in terms of content as in thanksgiving, intercession, supplication, adoration, and confession. Increasingly, some of us think about prayer in terms of its universal presence in the human being and its inevitable effect or consequence upon the pray-er, regardless of who or where she or he is. That is, we increasingly realize that as human beings we are, or become, like unto that to which we pray, or believe we are praying.

The Study of Prayer in Reformation Tradition

By and large, however, it is fairly safe to say that over the last five centuries of Reformation rationalism and enlightenment in first-world culture, there has been a considerable amount of pastoral (and even a good deal of inane) writing about prayer, but remarkably little about it as a proper subject for serious study or investigation. This avoidance of engagement has been particularly marked in the last century or so and seems to arise,

* Portions of this essay were first delivered as the Ingram Lectures at Memphis Theological Seminary on Reformation Day, 2007.

at least in part, from a kind of scorning of prayer as worthy of formal study.

A decade and a half ago, in a now-famous paper entitled "The Rhetoric of Supplication," Cynthia E. Garrett of Wells College in New York exposed to public view the investigative, theoretical, and theological wasteland to which the study of prayer *per se* had been assigned by mainstream Protestant scholarship in this country, especially during the 20th century. First quoting Professor Sam Gill's 1986 deadly summation of the disciplined study of prayer as being "undeveloped and naive,"[1] Garrett went on to proffer two explanations of her own for the West's peculiar want, over the last two or three centuries, of academic interest in the study of prayer as a human phenomenon: "Those religiously inclined," she said, "perhaps consider prayer beyond criticism, while students of intellectual and religious history may consider it somehow beneath criticism."[2]

Garrett even expanded her comments—that is, she drove the nail home, so to speak—by saying that while "manuals offering detailed instructions in private prayer were both a distinctive and highly popular form of post-Reformation English literature," they too have received little academic attention. This, she explains by saying:

> Because they—that is, Protestant prayer books and books about
> the practice of prayer—provide popular instruction rather than
> doctrine, they have escaped the notice of students of theology;
> because they rarely treat sectarian issues, they have proved of little
> interest to historians of religion . . . .[3]

The Times are A-changin': Emergent/Emerging Christianity

Garrett was correct, of course. Unfortunately, her observations continue to be apropos in the twenty-first century; for the academic and professional prejudices she described still hold in many seminaries and universities today. More to the point—and quite probably as a direct result of academic abnegation—those prejudices currently are very operative

---

1. Sam D. Gill, "Prayer," in *The Encyclopedia of Religion* (1986) 11:489, as quoted by Garrett, cf. note 3 below.

2. Cynthia E. Garrett, "The Rhetoric of Supplication: Prayer Theory in Seventeenth Century England," *Renaissance Quarterly* 46 (1993) 328.

3. Ibid.

in, and informing of, many Roman and Protestant pastorates. However, as the old song reminds us, "the times they are a-changin.'" Both Roman Catholicism and Protestantism (and to some extent Orthodoxy) are having to make way for another, vibrant stream in the flowing centuries of Christianity and Christian thought: emergent/emerging Christianity.

Emergent or emerging Christianity is exactly what its name implies. It is that set of religious sensibilities—cultural, theological and devotional—that are currently coalescing into a new, old way of being Church. The current, emergent embrace of radical Christianity, with its emphasis on the canonical Jesus and in its emphasis on joyful, communal, disciplined living, is forging—indeed, is morphing into—the corpus of that stream of Christian thought and praxis that undoubtedly will hold hegemony or pride of place among us over the next few centuries. And within that corpus of thought and praxis, nothing, absolutely nothing, is as central to it all as is prayer. As a result, in speaking of prayer in our time, we can indeed speak of it as a frontier. As we do so, however, we always must bear in mind that, especially in the English-speaking world, almost all of us—emergent or Protestant or Roman or Orthodox or other—come into the conversation with a kind of innocent or untutored paucity of phenomenological, theological and ecclesial information about prayer. Ironically, that paucity and innocence seem to have the substantial advantage of leaving us unencumbered and receptive when we come to conversations about prayers. There may be a concomitant disadvantage, of course, in a sheer lack of economy in our effort.

Post-Enlightment, Post-Modernist Critique of Prayer

When speaking of prayer as a frontier in our time and about our new interest in exploring the limits of it, we—be we emergence Christians or otherwise—must begin by recognizing that we belong to a time that is still self-defined and self-described by what we are not. That is, we say with complete ease of observation that we are post-denominational, post-modern, post-literate, post-Protestant, post-Reformation, post-Christendom, post-rational, etc. And when we rattle off all the "posts" that we commonly use to describe ourselves and our time, we always include "post-Enlightenment" as one of the major ones. Intuitively, we recognize that whether we be inherited Church or new and forming Church, a part of what is going on now among all our member-parts and communions is a reaction to the headiness, the overly intellectualized approach, of the Enlightenment as it attempted to reform the ossifying theology of the Reformation itself.

In his recently-released meditation on the Lord's Prayer, Telford Work summarizes the deficiencies of prayer in an Enlightenment culture by saying:

> If eternity lies within the world's own reach, why bother to pray for the Kingdom to come? God helps those who help themselves! In a world of progress, prayer becomes inspiration, encouragement, and introspection—a formality before an action already decided. A culture that takes matters into its own hands prays to a God of its own making, and before long, only to itself.[4]

The point of far greater pertinence, however, is that in the course of the twentieth-century culture out of which we are emerging, Enlightenment thought matured into modernist thought; and it is this heritage, in particular, that we are most driven to push through and beyond.

The late Robert Funk, the founder of The Jesus Seminar, was one of the twentieth century's most influential religionists; and we in the twenty-first century owe a great debt to him. Because he understood the power, within modernity, of publicity and star-quality prominence, Funk managed to call into public question the true role of historicity in Christianity, and indeed in religion itself. As modernity lay moribund in the last decade of the last century, Funk produced what was probably the quintessential summation or maturation or distillate of modernist theology, including its understanding of prayer.

In a paper entitled "The Coming Radical Reformation—Twenty-one Theses" and published in 1998, Funk listed as Thesis Number Five in his list of the givens of modernist Christianity this statement:

> Prayer is meaningless when understood as requests addressed to an external God for favor or forgiveness and meaningless if God does not interfere with the laws of nature. Prayer as praise is a remnant of the age of kingship in the ancient Near East and is beneath the dignity of deity. Prayer should be understood principally as meditation—as listening rather than talking—and as attention to the needs of neighbor.[5]

4. Telford Work, *Ain't Too Proud to Beg* (Grand Rapids: Eerdmans, 2007) 66.

5. *The Fourth R* 11:4 (July/August). Online at http://www.polebridgepress.com/Periodicals/4R_Articles/funk_theses.html.

In that same year of 1998, another prominent, popular theologian of modernist Christianity, also a member of The Jesus Seminar, Bishop Jack Spong, published a major work entitled *Why Christianity Must Change or Die*. Bishop Spong simultaneously issued over the World Wide Web a rather dramatic declaration titled "A Call for A New Reformation: Twelve Theses," which was drawn from the conclusions of his book.[6] In Bishop Spong's list, prayer comes in as Number Ten. His statement is far more succinct than is Funk's:

> Prayer can not be a request made to a theistic deity to act in human history in a particular way.

What Funk and Spong and other, sometimes less publicly-visible, theologians were doing, of course, was sensing and interpreting, quite accurately, first the ground tremors and then the tectonic shifts that have opened up twenty-first-century Christianity into new, post-Enlightenment ways of being. And in doing so, they became summarizers, more than prophets, recorders as it were, of the last, great gasps of a dying age. But what they also did was furnish us, in perfect specimen, the corpus of understanding and practice that we now are—and must be—in the business of unseating; and nowhere is that frontier crossing out of modernism more revelatory than it is when we speak of prayer.

Crossing Borders: Fixed-Hour Prayer

Every border crossing has a kind of history or genesis to it. It moves, like a subterranean process, from stasis to an awareness of some "other" that might be better, to thinking more and more about the qualities of the other, to thinking about the business of actually crossing over with all its inherent gains and losses, to innocently checking out the border's borders, and then at last to finally stepping over. It has been that way with us as we push farther into an understanding of prayer in these post-Enlightenment, post-Reformation times of ours.

Perhaps the most dramatic moment in our progressive push toward a renewed and/or greater understanding of prayer was not a moment at

---

6. Bishop Spong first released The Twelve Theses in the diocesan newspaper of the Episcopal Diocese of Newark, *The Voice* (May, 1998), and later published them in his book, *Here I Stand: My Struggle for a Christianity of Integrity, Love, and Equality* (San Francisco: HarperSanFrancisco, 2000) 453–54.

all, but rather consumed the better part of a decade. The mid- to late years of the 1990's through the opening two or three years of this century were those of our "stepping over;" and we did it in a most ancient and elegant way. We Western Christians returned—by the thousands, in fact—to fixed-hour prayer. We set aside our rational headiness and picked up, almost by blind intuition, the historic discipline of observing the hours or, as some call it, of saying the offices.

Scot McKnight, the Karl A. Olsson Professor of Religious Studies at North Park University, is an Anabaptist theologian by tradition; but, he also is widely acknowledged today as a deep and influential thinker within emergence Christianity. It was McKnight who first defined for post-moderns the distinction that accrues between praying *in* church and praying *with* the Church.[7] In making this distinction McKnight is teaching us that the time part of space/time is a mystery. He is attesting as well to the truth that there is a necessary and functioning communion, in and through time, not only with God, but also with the whole body of our fellow-Christians, both present and past.

One of the more or less inevitable consequences of keeping fixed-hour prayer, with its unrelenting schedule of interruption every three hours for prayer, is a primal, subtle, compelling, but certainly *not* enlightened, conviction. That conviction comes at first to the new practitioner as an uneasy awareness. That is, while the Abrahamic discipline of fixed-hour prayer may start as a mental exercise of intention, such prayer does not remain resident in the mind. Nor, for that matter, does it necessarily function in relationship to any of the sensory and intellectual information the brain may be synthesizing for, and furnishing to, the self.

Rather, the offices increasingly come to "feel" as if they are resident in, and informed by, some part of the human being for which Western Christianity seems to have no real name other than that of "heart." And being present in, or resident in, the "heart," when that word is left unexamined as a term, can become vague and unsatisfactory.

Over the centuries, Orthodox Christianity has been more intentional than we in the West in its refining of a theology and typography of interior and prayer experience. One of Orthodoxy's complaints against Western Christianity since the Great Schism, in fact, has been our cavalier use of "heart" as shorthand for something we are too lazy to wrestle

7. Scot McKnight, *Praying With the Church* (Brewster, MA: Paraclete, 2005).

with and define. All of this, of course, brings us to the sure recognition that somewhere along the way we did indeed cross a border and have now emerged into frontier country.

Post-Modern Christians and the "I" That Prays

Ours certainly is not the first time of re-configuration, of breaking new ground and entering new territory. The Great Schism of a thousand years ago was itself such a period, as was the Great Reformation that gave the Church Protestantism five hundred years after that. Each time there has been such a period of re-configuration, there is also the same, central question: Where now is our authority?

At the same time, each period of such re-adjustment and change has always had one or two questions that are either peculiar to itself and its own period of time and culture, or else recurring ones in human experience. For us today, one major recurring question is that of consciousness. For the first time in several centuries, we no longer know "who" is thinking when we think, or even "think" that we are thinking. We understand today, in the way that earlier eras did not, that the brain is a biological organ that can be seen, cut apart, stimulated and then observed in action. We understand as well that it translates chemical signals into actions or data, only some of which eventuate not only in an action or re-action, but also in the supra-action we name as consciousness. Just who or what it is that perceives such awareness and even is capable of naming it as well as remembering and/or employing it remains for us considerably less clear, often dangerously so. Our on-going contentiousness with one another about abortion, for instance, feeds to a large extent on our lack of clarity about what is and is not "human" when and in relation to what. So do end-of-life issues which daily become more painful and more embittering for all participants in the debates. Beyond that, there are the less immediately incarnate, more academic questions, such as, "What precisely is mind in relation to brain?" "What is intellect?" "What even is the *nous* of the philosophers and of Orthodox Christianity?"

Increasingly over the last decade or so, cognitive science and neuro-biologists and consciousness theorists have come to dominate the covers and feature stories of popular magazines, the talk-shows and, of late, even the more popular blogs, with a veritable barrage of just such questions, ones that they as experts raise, but unfortunately can not yet answer. For post-modernist Christians, those cultural, ethical, and scientific questions have become increasingly condensed into one, very focused question, namely, "'What' is it that prays when 'I' go to my prayers?"

Is there really a "self" that is resident in human biology, but not subject to dissection, being a sum greater than its parts, yet loosed or unmoored by the violation of any one of them? Most Western Christians, unless they happen to be cognitive scientists or cyber-theorists, would say, "Yes," to that question without a great deal of thought. Yes, there is such a unity or unit, the majority of us would say; and then probably say as well that, after the flesh's death, the evidence of that unity lives on in the effects it has had within creation and upon creation's memory. Meanwhile the soul, we would venture very Plato-like, is not so much the self's immortal twin as it is the self's vitality that escapes space/time upon the flesh's demise.

Many cognitive scientists, physicists, and cyber-theorists are vociferously and ubiquitously and sometimes persuasively less sure. More and more Christians are hearing them, and hearing them not as dissidents, but as adventurers coming back with promising tales about inhabited lands beyond the frontier itself. The effect of these promising tales suggest a typology of prayer far less inane than, for instance, traditionally Western ones like that of ordering by content (as in adoration, confession, thanksgiving, supplication, and intercession); or by method or attitude of approach (as in centering, contemplative, meditative, ecstatic, or breath prayer); or by venue and form (like corporate or private, rote and liturgical, fixed and spontaneous). The reports suggest instead, the possibility of a typology by area or mode of effect, a typology that, because it can bear up to studied consideration, may sift out the holy from the ordinary, the mysterious from the naturally explicable, in prayer. That distillation to pure or unmediated prayer is of the greatest importance for 21st century Christians and Western Christianity, as it must also be for Christians of any persuasion alive in today's world.

Conversations about Prayer: Six Categories of Interest

Beyond question, it is much too early in the current process for any of us to predict with surety where our re-invigorated lay, academic, and clerical interest in the typology, theology, and phenomenology of prayer will lead North Americans, and especially North American Christians, over the coming decades. All any of us can be sure about just now is that the interest and the questions are pervasive and that the ball indisputably is in motion. That having been acknowledged, it is still possible, for purposes of discussion, to suggest that most conversations about prayer can be catalogued into one or more of six categories of interest or perspectives:

- *Prayer as it may be considered physiologically:* that is, prayer as a largely subjective but efficacious work that is open to all people without regard to religious belief or lack thereof; that exercises an intuitive sense of being within some larger self or intention and/or of control; that evokes scientifically demonstrable activity within the subject; and that, minimally, grants certain, again demonstrable, benefits of well-being to the individual pray-er;

- *Prayer as it may be considered kinesthetically:* that is, prayer as an agent of change, and perhaps even choice, in physical actualities, with particular interest in the means by which such change is, first, measured and, second, effected;

- *Prayer as it may be considered liturgically:* that is, prayer as a part of formalized worship within a tradition, whether offered corporately, individually, or in non-locative unity, but which is always formative, with especial emphasis on the unity of experience this form of prayer offers and on its efficacy as an instrument of cohesiveness;

- *Prayer as it may be considered conjunctively:* that is, prayer as the principal network of communication with our own, albeit undefined, selves and of communication both among us who are within space/time, and also with and among those agencies and selves outside of it;

- *Prayer as it may be considered conductively:* that is, prayer as a means of opening the pray-er to become a conduit back into space/time of either the healing beneficence of the Holy or (we must not ignore this) the damning force of the Unholy;

- *Prayer as it may be considered generatively:* that is, prayer as the discipline that liberates the soul from the persona in much the same way that hatching frees the chick from the confines of its shell, thereby releasing it into a frame of reference beyond itself.

The six categories are not mutually exclusive, of course, nor do they constitute an exhaustive typology of prayer *in toto*, but rather of the current discussion about it *in situ*. The categories or perspectives, likewise, can blend with one another within the confines of any single or discrete prayer act. But we must, none the less, acknowledge that the very existence of a discernible, reconstituted (perhaps even new) typology of prayer by site of effect or conduct is opening the way, within our time, for the serious, distinguished, and strenuous study of prayer in a manner that has not appertained for many, many years, if indeed ever, in North American Christian experience or scholarship.

There is, patent in all this, also an imperative in our time for Christianity to once more honor her own progeny by beginning to hold sustained and respectful, open and receptive, conversations with secular science. Nowhere is that conversation more urgent or more potentially fruitful than it is where prayer is concerned. Post-modern Christianity, almost by definition, demands that the mechanisms of prayer be separated out and sorted—that is, that the kinesthetic and physiologically objectively explicable be lifted out from the not objectively explicable and reproducible—that the processes of prayer be demystified in order that the great Mystery may be the better seen and served—that the path in be weeded and the trash hauled away and dumped, so to speak.

Beyond that, we should direct particular attention here, even if just briefly, to Category Six, that of generative prayer. The present answers to today's consuming questions about the nature of mind as opposed to brain, or of consciousness as distinct from intellect, or of cognitive modification and simulations and enhancements in general, will, in a century, seem rather quaint, I suspect. That is, they will come, over the next cache of decades, to appear as inadequate and antique as Rene Descartes's *cogito ergo sum* is to us today. The emerging new corpus of Christianity and of those Christians who are forming it recognize that fact just as surely as do the rest of us; but what they also contend—passionately, assertively, graphically—is that by whatever name or names we finally end up calling all our energetic parts, there is and always has been a conduit—a channel of luminous bathing, a non-locative and generative place—where aliveness meets and knows undiluted Aliveness and is re-created or re-assembled by it—where generation happens and is on-going.

There is a something or somewhere—call it "heart" for now, if we must—where clarity is imageless and soundless and pedagogical, a chamber within or of the human creature where the eye does indeed become the lamp of the body and the whole is thereby flooded. There, in that circumstance, is the consummate meeting of the fire and the rose, to use Eliot's naming of it, or a form of *theoria*, to use that of our Orthodox brothers and sisters. By whatever name, however, when we speak of prayer generatively, what we are saying is as simple as humility itself. "There is a road in," we are saying, "which is paved by continuous use and we are vowed to follow it."

It behooves each of us, then, in whatever else we do, to honor that endeavor. The Christianity of the next half a millennium is being sculpted even as we calmly read these and thousands of other words about it; and in no other component or part of religion are the stakes so high today as they are in prayer, for—and here truly is the point—for we really are as we pray, and we border-crossers really will become as we believe and understand the frontier to be.

The Powers and Christian Eucharistic Prayer

L. Edward Phillips

> In genuine worship the Christian assembly celebrates the sover-
> eign rule of the God of Jesus Christ over the nations, institutions,
> and systems of the world, over human history, and over the entire
> Creation.
>
> —GENE DAVENPORT[1]

The Great Thanksgiving of the United Methodist Order of Word and
Table contains the following bit of historic, catholic liturgy:

> And so, with your people on earth, and all the company of heav-
> en, we praise your name, and join their unending hymn: Holy,
> holy, holy Lord, God of power and might, heaven and earth are
> full of your glory. . . .

While I doubt that Methodists always consider what they are saying in
this prayer, the ramifications are stunning. We do not make worship happen in our local congregations. Rather, we join in what is already taking
place, around the world and in heaven.

The hymn we join to sing is the *Sanctus*, the angelic song of praise
that Isaiah heard in the temple when he had his vision of God in heaven:

> Seraphs were in attendance above him; each had six wings: with
> two they covered their faces, and with two they covered their
> feet, and with two they flew. And one called to another and said:
> "Holy, holy, holy is the LORD of hosts; the whole earth is full of
> his glory." (Isa 6:2–3)[2]

---

1. *Powers and Principalities* (Cleveland: Pilgrim, 2003) 49.
2. All references are to the NRSV.

The angelic hosts cover their faces and bodies before the glory of God, for even Seraphs are modest in the Divine Presence. The Revelation of John records a similar vision of heavenly praise, with four six-winged creatures representing various orders of animals (domestic animals, wild beasts, birds, and human beings), all singing before the throne of God: "Day and night without ceasing they sing. 'Holy, holy, holy, the Lord God, the Almighty, who was and is, and is to come'" (Rev 4:8). This is a vision of perpetual worship of the hosts of heaven before God. The angelic beings are not the only ones that offer praise, however. Those who have suffered through the great tribulation, who have washed their robes "in the blood of the Lamb," also worship God "day and night within his temple" (Rev 7:15). When, in our Eucharistic prayer, Christians join with "the entire company of heaven," we have joined in a cosmic, liturgical celebration that transcends time and space, and that acknowledges and celebrates the Power of God who is sovereign over the created Powers of heaven and earth. Whether we realize it or not, the Lord's Supper (Holy Communion, the Eucharist) is about the alignment of power, the submission of the Powers of heaven and earth before the Lord of Creation.

Power and Eucharist in the New Testament

The biblical theology of "the Powers" has been a central theme in Gene Davenport's teaching and writing. In his book, *Principalities and Powers*, he describes the Powers as:

1. God's creatures

2. that are transcendent beings (meaning not subject to time or space)

3. that are embodied in our world as systems, ideologies, governments (and people),

4. that are good by virtue of creation,

5. but fallen and corrupt (driven toward self-preservation)

6. yet, still beneficial to the world insofar as they fulfill their created purpose to serve God by ordering the world for the flourishing of God's creation.[3]

---

3. *Principalities and Powers*, 11–13.

Through an examination of representative historical texts, I want to show that, from the earliest times, Christians have understood the Eucharist to be an engagement with these cosmic, transcendent Powers.

Paul, who records the earliest glimpse of the Christian practice of the Lord's Supper in 1 Corinthians, provides a clue to the cosmic significance of the meal:

> Therefore, my dear friends, flee from the worship of idols. . . .The cup of blessing that we bless, is it not a sharing in the blood of Christ? The bread that we break, is it not a sharing in the body of Christ? Because there is one bread, we who are many are one body, for we all partake of the one bread. Consider the people of Israel; are not those who eat the sacrifices partners in the altar? What do I imply then? That the food sacrificed to idols is anything, or that an idol is anything? No, I imply that what pagans sacrifice, they sacrifice to demons and not to God. I do not want you to be partners with demons. You cannot drink the cup of the Lord and the cup of demons. You cannot partake of the table of the Lord and the table of demons. (1 Cor 14–21)

According to Paul, the Lord's Supper is a fellowship meal with cosmic power ramifications: in the supper we have fellowship (sharing, *koinonia*) with Christ that parallels pagan sacrifices by which one becomes a partner (*koinonos*) with demons, spiritual powers that are counter to God. The contrast is absolute: one cannot have fellowship with both demons and the Lord.

Yet even the avoidance of pagan sacrifice *per se* does not guarantee a fruitful participation in the Lord's Supper. In chapter 11, Paul denounces the wealthier Christians in Corinth who are free to come to the fellowship meals early and eat the food before the working class, and poorer, members of the church arrive:

> When you come together, it is not really to eat the Lord's supper. For when the time comes to eat, each of you goes ahead with your own supper, and one goes hungry and another becomes drunk. (1 Cor 11:20–21)

The Corinthians have failed to manifest the body of Christ in their structural life because they dishonor the most vulnerable in the community ("those who have nothing," v. 22). Paul reminds them that the Lord's Supper is eschatological, anticipating the final revelation of Christ: "For as often as you eat this bread and drink the cup, you proclaim the Lord's death until he comes" (1 Cor 11:26). The Lord's Supper must not (Paul suggests, *cannot*) be a community ritual that reiterates the social divisions of culture; rather, it is an eschatological enactment of Church as the Body of Christ (as described in 1 Cor 12). The Lord's Supper fundamentally entails discernment of the radical, counter-cultural structure of the Body of Christ, and the judgment that this brings upon the world: "For all who eat and drink without discerning the body [i.e., the church as the body of Christ] eat and drink judgment against themselves" (v. 29). In short, the Corinthians may not have understood what they were doing (v. 20), but that does not change what the Lord's Supper must do to them—discipline them into a corporate body that is different from the power-structures of the world.

Power at the Eucharist in the Early Second Century

Roughly fifty years after Paul wrote to the Corinthians, Bishop Ignatius of Antioch describes the regular gathering for worship as a confrontation with the powers of Satan:

> Be eager, then, to meet more often for thanksgiving [*eucharistia*] and glory [*doxa*] to God; for when you come together often, the powers [*dunameis*] of Satan are broken, and his destructiveness is shattered by the concord of your faith. Nothing is better than peace, by which all warfare of heavenly and earthly beings is destroyed.[4]

Bishop Ignatius, who wrote his letters while being transported under armed guard to Rome for trial and (according to tradition) martyrdom, describes peace within the Christian community as a sort of war against war: by peace, war is destroyed. Satan's power is broken by the concord (*homonoia*, literally, "oneness of mind") of the community at worship, which is a meeting for giving thanks (that is, literally, *eucharistia*, a term Ignatius explicitly uses for the ritual meal in his *Letter to the Philadelphians*) and giving glory to God.

---

4. *Letter to the Ephesians* 13:1–2. The translation is William R. Schoedel, *Ignatius of Antioch: A Commentary on the Letters of Ignatius of Antioch* (Philadelphia: Fortress, 1985) 74.

This association of *eucharistia* (thanksgiving) with *doxa* (glory) at the Lord's Supper did not originate with Ignatius. *The Didache,* a church order that dates from the late first to early second century C.E.[5] provides two prayers for a Eucharist, one to be said before (chapter 9) and one after (chapter 10) the ritual meal. Both of these prayers begin with a call to give thanks (they are, literally, "eucharistic"), and both of these prayers are constructed of three distinct paragraphs, each of which concludes with an attribution of glory to God. For example, here is the first strophe of the prayer in *Did.* 10:2:

> We thank You, holy Father, for Your holy name which You did cause to tabernacle in our hearts, and for the knowledge and faith and immortality, which You made known to us through Jesus Your Servant [or Child, *paidon*]; *to You be the glory for ever.*[6]

The third strophe expands on this concluding attribution of glory to God as illustrated by *Did.* 10:5:

> Remember, Lord, Your Church, to deliver it from all evil and to make it perfect in Your love, and gather it from the four winds, sanctified for Your kingdom which You have prepared for it; *for Yours is the power and the glory for ever.*[7]

This expanded conclusion adds the recognition of God's power, and mirrors the standard concluding formula for the Lord's Prayer.

The middle strophe of this prayer (*Did.* 10:3–4) recognizes God as creator and giver of gifts, both physical and spiritual:

> You, Master almighty, created all things for Your name's sake; You gave food and drink to humankind for enjoyment, that they might give thanks to You; but to us You did freely give spiritual food and drink and life eternal through Your Servant. Before all things, we thank You because You are powerful [*dunatos*]; to You be the glory for ever.

---

5. Credible dates for material contained in *The Didache* range from the middle of the first century to the early second century. See Kurt Niederwimmer, *The Didache* (Minneapolis: Fortress, 1998) 52–54.

6. Translation adapted, *Ante-Nicene Fathers* (Peabody, MA: Hendrickson, 1995 [orig. ed., 1886]) 1:380; emphasis added.

7. Ibid.

Since Louis Finkelstein's work on this prayer in the early twentieth century, many scholars have considered the Eucharistic prayers in *The Didache* to be Christianized versions of Jewish table blessings, such as the *Birkat ha-mazon,* the standard Jewish blessing after a meal.[8] Yet the Jewish *Birkat ha-mazon* makes no obvious reference to divine or cosmic power. The parallel passages of the *Birkat ha-mazon* and *Did.* 10:4 demonstrate this contrast. The Jewish blessing reads: "For all these things we give thanks to you and praise your name for ever and ever."[9] *Did.* 10.4 reads: "For all these things we thank you *because you are powerful*" (emphasis added). While the *Didache* does not explicitly describe the Eucharist as a confrontation with the powers of Satan as we find in Ignatius, nevertheless, the Eucharist is not simply praise of God as the giver of good things; it is also very much about the recognition of divine glory and power.[10]

Power and the Eucharist in the Mid-second Century: Justin Martyr

Around the year 160 C.E., the apologist Justin Martyr, writing from Rome, makes explicit the connection of the Eucharist and the overthrowing of the destructive powers. In the *Dialogue with Trypho, a Jew,* Justin lists several Old Testament types (or figures) for Christ (for example, the Passover Lamb is a figure of Christ) before arriving at this description of Eucharistic prayer:

> And the offering of fine flour, sirs, I said, which was prescribed to
> be presented on behalf of those purified from leprosy, was a type
> of the bread of the Eucharist, the celebration of which our Lord
> Jesus Christ prescribed, in remembrance of the suffering which

8. "The Birkat Ha-Mazon," *Jewish Quarterly Review* 19 (1928/1929) 211–62. The connection has recently been challenged by Paul Bradshaw, *Eucharistic Origins* (New York: Oxford University Press, 2004) 32–35. Among the problems is that no early Jewish text of the *Birkat ha-mazon* exists, and Finkelstein has to read back from much later (well after the 4th century) texts to reconstruct a first century *Birkat ha-mazon* by extracting the Christian material.

9. From Finkelstein's text of the *Birkat ha-mazon* as quoted in Bradshaw, *Eucharist Origins,* 33.

10 Gene Davenport's first book, based on his dissertation, is *Eschatology of the Book of Jubilees* (Leiden: Brill, 1971). I cannot resist noting that *Jubilees* 22:6–9 contains a prayer with some parallels to the *Birkat ha-mazon.* Yet, there is not a hint of power language in this prayer. I do not have the space, here, to discuss the apocalyptic conclusion to the *Didache* (ch. 16).

He endured on behalf of those who are purified in soul from all iniquity, in order that we may at the same time thank God for having created the world, with all things therein, for the sake of man, and for delivering us from the evil in which we were, and for utterly overthrowing principalities and powers by Him who suffered according to His will.[11]

According to Justin, the Eucharist is performed as a memorial of Christ's suffering for us, and, "at the same time," a thanksgiving for creation, for salvation, and for "utterly overthrowing principalities and powers." The phrase here translated "utterly overthrowing" in Greek is *katalelukenai teleian katalusin*, literally, "having overthrown with perfect overthrow." This may be an allusion to Col 2:15: "He [Christ] disarmed the rulers and authorities [i.e., Principalities and Powers] and made a public example of them, triumphing over them in it [i.e., the cross]."[12]

In his various surviving works, Justin Martyr displays an understanding of angels and demons that is based on the Old Testament, but he also draws on Jewish angelology found in extra-canonical literature. In this system of interpretation, angels were originally created by God to take care of the human race. Some of the angels, however, participated in the fall (Justin cites Gen 6:1–4, the account of the Nephilim, as his example). The fallen angels and demons (which are children of the fallen) now lead human beings into sin: "murders, wars, adulteries, intemperate deeds, and all wickedness."[13] These fallen angels and demons are the spiritual powers that the pagans mistake for "gods," and they are hostile to the worship of the true God of the Bible.[14] Thus, Justin represents what will become a fairly standard early Christian explanation for the existence of pagan deities, one that draws on various Jewish sources, but also on the letters of Paul.[15]

This passage from Justin fits more closely with the realized eschatology of Colossians and Ephesians, rather than the more reserved eschatology of 1 Corinthians 15:24–28, where the destruction of the Principalities and Powers has yet to be fully manifest. There may also be a

11. *Dialogue with Trypho* 41 (trans. *Ante-Nicene Fathers*, 1:215).

12. The Greek word for "disarmed" is *apekdusamenos*, rather than *katalelukenai*. This does not seem to be a direct quotation of Colossians, but an allusion.

13. *Second Apology* 5.

14. *Dial. Trypho* 30.

15. E.g. 1 Cor. 10:20.

difference between Justin's understanding of the relationship of Eucharist and the Powers and that of Ignatius, cited above. For Ignatius, the church actively participates in the "breaking of the powers of Satan" through the manifestation of harmony in the eucharistic assembly. For Justin, at the Eucharist, the church gives thanks for the overthrowing of the Powers that is already accomplished in the cross. These differences aside, the association of the Eucharist with the defeat of the Powers is central to both of these early Christian writers.

The Third Century: The Apostolic Tradition

The brief description of the Eucharist provided by Justin suggests the content of a second-century Eucharistic prayer that contains these elements: an acknowledgement of Christ's atoning work on the cross, thanksgiving for creation, and recognition of the victory over the powers of evil. The so-called *Apostolic Tradition of Hippolytus* provides an example of what a Eucharistic prayer may have sounded like in Justin's congregation. Following the opening dialogue ("The Lord be with you," etc.), the thanksgiving continues:

> We render thanks to you, God, through your beloved child [or servant, Latin: *puer*] Jesus Christ, whom in the last times you sent to us as savior and redeemer and angel of your will, who is your inseparable word, through whom you made all things and it was well-pleasing to you; you sent from heaven into the virgin's womb, and who conceived in the womb was incarnate and manifested as your son, born of the holy spirit and the virgin; who fulfilling your will and gaining for you a holy people stretched out [his] hands when he was suffering, that he might release from suffering those who believed in you; *who when he was being handed over to voluntary suffering, that he might destroy death and break the bonds of the devil, and tread down hell and illuminated the righteous, and fix a limit and manifest the resurrection* [emphasis added], taking bread [and] giving things to you, he said: "Take, eat, this is my body which will be broken for you." Likewise also the cup, saying: "This is my blood which is shed for you [etc.]"[16]

16. *Apostolic Tradition*, 38, 40. Translation from Paul F. Bradshaw, Maxwell E. Johnson, and L. Edward Phillips, *The Apostolic Tradition* (Minneapolis: Fortress, 2002) 38, 40. Text amended for illustration purposes. This important early church order can no longer with confidence be attributed to the third-century Roman theologian Hippolytus.

This prayer is dramatically different from the Eucharistic prayers in *The Didache*, and more like Eucharistic prayers in the later catholic tradition. It is thoroughly Christological; even the thanksgiving for creation is configured through Christ, "through whom you [God] made all things." The thanksgiving moves in narrative summary from the sending of Christ, to creation through him, to the incarnation, to the passion. The cosmic significance of the passion is succinctly described ("that he might destroy death, and break the bonds of the devil, and tread down hell . . .") before giving an account of the institution of the Eucharist. The progression is jarring, moving from the cosmic defeat of the devil to the domestic setting of the Last Supper.[17] Even so, this seems to be what Justin described. In following Jesus' prescription to celebrate the Lord's Supper as a memorial of his suffering, Christians are, *at the same time*, thanking God for creation, for delivering us from evil, and for defeating the powers that enslave the world. While the Eucharistic prayer in the *Apostolic Tradition* does not explicitly use the language of "Principalities and Powers," it enacts a feast of thanksgiving celebrating the victory of Christ, in his cross and resurrection, over death and the "bonds of the devil."

Power and Eucharist in the Fourth Century: A Constantinian Shift?

To summarize the argument thus far: from its origin through the third-century witnesses, the Christian Eucharist was viewed as an acknowledgement of God's power over the world, and, at the same time, as a celebration of victory over the fallen Principalities and Powers that challenge God's dominion. Following the peace of Constantine, and the gradual end of state persecution in the Roman Empire, Christian prayers will begin to display a more favorable role for the "Principalities and Powers" in the Eucharist.

In the fourth century we have, for the first time, examples of Eucharistic prayers that include the *Sanctus* similar to the *Sanctus* of con-

---

See Bradshaw, Johnson, Phillips, *Apostolic Tradition*, 2–6.

17. This is, arguably, the earliest example we have of the institution narrative inserted into a Eucharistic prayer. Some scholars suggest that the narrative was added to this prayer in the mid-fourth century. See Bradshaw, Johnson, Phillips, *Apostolic Tradition*, 45–46. Even if we accept a late date for the insertion of the institution narrative, this does not change the point that the meal itself is an enactment of the victory of Christ over the devil.

temporary Eucharistic prayers.[18] The *Sanctus* is invariably preceded by an introduction that identifies the angelic voices that sing the hymn. The earliest example of this is found in a fourth-century Eucharistic prayer from Egypt that is attributed to Sarapion of Thmuis (a bishop and acquaintance of Athanasius, the champion of Nicene orthodoxy). Here is the relevant portion of the prayer:

> For you are far above every principality and power and virtue and dominion and every name that is named, not only in this age but in the age to come.
> Beside you stand thousands of thousands and myriads of myriads of angels, archangels, thrones, dominions, principalities, and powers. Beside you stand the two most honorable seraphim with six wings, which cover the face with two wings, and the feet with two, and fly with two; and they cry, "Holy," with them receive also our cry of "Holy," as we say: "Holy, holy, holy, Lord of Sabaoth; heaven and earth are full of you glory."[19]

This prayer asserts the rule of God over the powers, as in the earlier witnesses. But rather than proclaiming the defeat of the powers, in Sarapion's thanksgiving the Principalities and Powers stand beside God along with the two seraphim who sing "Holy, holy, holy."

The eucharistic prayer found in the late fourth-century *Apostolic Constitutions* has a similar introduction to the *Sanctus*:

> You are worshipped . . . by unnumbered armies of angels, archangels, thrones, dominions, principalities, powers, virtues, eternal armies. The cherubim and seraphim with two wings covering their feet, with two their heads, and with two flying, together with thousands of thousands of archangels and myriads of myriads of angels say unceasingly, never resting their voices: Holy, holy, holy, [etc.][20]

While the wording differs a little from the parallel in Sarapion, the fundamental concept is similar. The Principalities and Powers worship God along with the angels and archangels, and, by implication, join in their

---

18. There are various theories about the origin of the *Sanctus* in Eucharistic prayers, but there is no indisputable evidence that the *Sanctus* predates the fourth century.

19. Trans. from R. C. D. Jasper and G. J. Cuming, *Prayers of the Eucharist: Early and Reformed*, 3rd ed. revised (Collegeville, MN: Pueblo, 1987) 77.

20. Jasper and Cuming, *Prayers of the Eucharist*, 108–9.

angelic hymn. Virtually all other early Eucharistic prayers have a pre-*Sanctus* unit similar to these two examples.

I suggest the following conceptual evolution: in the second and third centuries, Christians understood the Eucharist either to enact the defeat of the Powers (Ignatius) or to be a celebration of the accomplishment of their defeat (Justin, the *Apostolic Tradition*). In the fourth century, the church recognized the Powers as eschatologically redeemed, fulfilling their created purpose and joining in the praise of God. It appears that the change of political climate under the emperor Constantine and his successors (the brief return to paganism under Julian, notwithstanding), led the church to offer a more positive evaluation of political power represented by the Principalities and Powers.

Eucharist and the Submission of the Powers

There is a conceptual danger in this "promotion" of the Powers. If the Powers are simply presented as already redeemed and offering praise with the seraphim, Christians may begin to think that the embodiment of these Powers in the world (the emperor and his armies, or my nation and its president) are already redeemed and worthy of full obedience as the authorities decreed by God. Christians have all-too-often accepted such a false understanding of the Powers.

Nevertheless, I do not believe that such a false understanding of the Powers is inevitable, because Christ's subduing of the Powers is simply not dependent upon human understanding of the fact. Christ's act precedes human understanding. Paul told the Corinthians that the Lord's Supper would not conform to their mistaken practice of it; rather, in the Supper Christ was shaping them into his body, a corporation that countered the social division of class, ethnicity, and even gender in the structures of the fallen world (1 Cor 12:13 and Gal 3:28). Paul warned the Corinthians to submit to the reality embodied (literally) in the Eucharist, and that warning still applies. Failure to discern this body of Christ is to remain in the condemnation of the world, where bodies are dominated by sickness and death ("For this reason many of you are weak and ill, and some have died" (1 Cor 11:29), rather than liberated for resurrection (1 Cor 15).

When United Methodist Christians, in harmony with the church throughout the ages, say at the Eucharist, "with your people on earth, and all the company of heaven we praise your name and join in their unending hymn," we are prompted to join with the holy angels in declaring the fullness of God's glory in heaven and earth. The great hymn does not require *our* voices, *our* consent, or even *our* understanding, for the heavenly hosts and the saints of God will sing it, nonetheless. Yet, whenever we earnestly join our voices, give our consent, and seek to understand, we hear in this prayer an invitation to holiness, and a judgment against all that would hinder our growth in holiness.

The Eucharist, moreover, is not primarily about the holiness of individual Christians. It is a supremely political act. We drag along the Principalities and Powers that cling to us as racism, sexism, nationalistic pride, class division, and all the structures of social, economic, and political domination. At the Eucharistic table, the Powers behold their defeat by the death and resurrection of Christ, in the presence of a human community of resistance to their domination—a community engaged in fellowship, breaking bread, sharing wine, repenting of sin, forgiving debts, honoring the poor, challenging the strong, empowering the weak, in the name of the Risen Lord. But beyond defeat, they also behold their created purpose and their ultimate redemption in Christ when the structures of domination will be re-created for the flourishing of creation, and they can take their place in the choir of the holy angels that sing of God's eternal glory.

Prairie Mysticism: An "Exegesis" of Bob Nolan's "Cool Water" and "Tumbling Tumbleweeds"

Tex Sample

Gene Davenport is an expert on the Sons of the Pioneers and I'm not. He is, moreover, a singer with CD recordings of their songs and I'm not. So it is with some trepidation that I undertake this "exegesis" of the two most famous of the Sons of the Pioneers' songs, Bob Nolan's "Cool Water" and "Tumbling Tumbleweeds." While I do have some history of studying country music, I have not focused as much on Western music.[1]

Still, I have loved the Sons of the Pioneers all my life. In my childhood and youth I went with great regularity to see Charles Starrett, Gene Autry, and Roy Rogers at the old Arcade, Haven and Dixie Theaters in Brookhaven, Mississippi. There I listened to Bob Nolan and the Sons of the Pioneers sing their wonderful songs. I dreamed of being a cowboy and riding the range. And when Gene or Roy sang with them, that was as good as it ever got.

At the time, I don't think I ever thought much about what the songs "said" except for some romantic sense in which they conveyed to me the adventure of cowboy life. I knew that Gene and Roy and the Sons were all good, and the outlaws were all bad. That was about all I needed to know. I didn't see desert and plains until I was fourteen years old, and even then from the window of a car on a trip to California.

I suppose, too, I was "ruined" by studying the Christian faith and belonging to the church. I began to read and understand the world from a perspective shaped by these two things and I have never been quite the same. So the church as a community of interpretation will form my work-

---

1. See my *White Soul* (Nashville: Abingdon, 1996).

ing with "Cool Water" and "Tumbling Tumbleweeds."[2] I make no apology for this, but I need to be clear that Bob Nolan did not see the world this way, at least from the little we know about him and his religious views.

Bob Nolan

A Canadian, Clarence Robert Nobles was born on April 13, 1908, in Midwestern Canada, in Winnipeg, Manitoba. He lived for a few years on the subsistence farm of his paternal grandparents. His father, Harry Bayard Nobles, was often gone, and his mother, Flora, left the family when Robert and his brother, Earle, were quite young.[3]

In 1919, when he was eleven years old, Nolan was sent to Boston to live with his aunts to obtain schooling, which had been hit and miss in the isolation of his Canadian home. It was here that he first came in contact with American folk music and was introduced to the poetry of Keats and Byron. Two years later, at the age of thirteen, Nolan went to Tucson, Arizona. He joined his father, who served stateside in the U.S. Army during World War I and moved to Tucson for health reasons. Harry Nobles likely suffered from the flu of 1918, which left him with chronic lung damage. Nobles changed the family name to Nolan when he enlisted in the army in 1917.

In Tucson, Bob Nolan for the first time experienced the desert in all of its majestic beauty. It had a profound impact on the way he saw the world:

2. See Stanley Fish, *Is There a Text in This Class* (Cambridge, MA: Harvard University Press, 1980). Fish makes the point that there is no such thing as reading a text without interpretation and that we read texts from within a community of interpretation.

3. For articles on Nolan's life see Ken Griffis, *Hear My Song: The Story of the Celebrated Sons of the Pioneers* (Northglenn, CO: Norken, 1998) 133–37; Kenneth J. Bindas, "Western Mystic: Bob Nolan and His Songs," *Western Historical Quarterly*, 17 (1986) 429–56; and Bill O'Neal and Fred Goodwin, *The Sons of the Pioneers* (Austin, TX: Eakin, 2001) passim. I have been especially helped by Elizabeth Drake MacDonald. She and Nolan's only grandson, Calin Coburn, have done more recent research and corrected important factual matters in Nolan's life. I have drawn from these in this account. My report here of Nolan's life reflects her corrections in an email to me on June 23, 2008.

I also want to express my genuine appreciation to Gene Davenport who offered fine counsel on Nolan and his music and provided the lyrics of songs and a number of other resources. I, of course, must take responsibility for what is finally here. I consulted with Davenport without letting him know that the paper was for his *Festschrift*, which was to be a surprise.

At first you see and hear nothing, then the desert becomes alive with things few people ever see. The desert and prairie country's first impact on me was an entirely new phase of life. You see, I was brought up in the back woods of Canada, and after World War I, I came to Tucson, Arizona, right from the tall timber, out to the desert. It was awe-inspiring, to say the least, to wake up in the morning to see the desert beauty with the sun shining through millions of drops of dew. It was just outstanding.[4]

His love affair with the desert and prairie would last the rest of his life. Nolan finished high school in Tucson and distinguished himself as a fine athlete in track and field, representing his school at the 1927 Arizona Track Meet.[5] While a sophomore in high school, he wrote the poem "Cool Water." It later became the well-known song by that title.

Nolan traveled almost incessantly from 1927–1929, making several trips to Mexico. Calling himself a "professional hobo," he traveled without any particular destination, but moved constantly between Florida and Arizona and "all towns in between." During these travels he first began to write Western songs.[6]

In 1928 he married a Tucson girl, Pearl Fields. She gave birth to their only child, Roberta. Nolan and Pearl, however, did not live together very long, and his daughter did not meet him until she was fifteen years old. Nolan's legal divorce from Pearl came some five years after her birth, although no documentation for the date of the divorce has been found.

Nolan claimed that in these years he attended the University of Arizona and studied musical harmony and construction there.[7] Contrary

---

4. Quoted in Griffis, *Hear My Song,* 133f.

5. Tucson High School Yearbook Staff, *The Tucsonian* (Tucson, 1927) 100. See Bindas, "Western Mystic," 443. Bindas reports that Nolan did not finish high school, because neither Nolan's name nor his photo appear in the 1928 yearbook. See ibid., 442n22. But Elizabeth MacDonald obtained a letter from the Custodian of Student Records in Tucson, Frederick Lenczycki, indicating that Nolan did, in fact, graduate. Email to me, June 23, 2008.

6. Bindas, "Western Mystic," 443.

7. Douglas B. Green Interview with Bob Nolan, November 20, 1979. Webite: www/ bobnolan-sop.net, June 20, 2008. The resultant story was printed on page 88 of *The Music City News*, January/February, 1980. The total interview is printed on www/bobnolan-sop.net. (The background song, *Relative Man*, is performed here by Jim Nabors.) This is the best website I found. It contains not only the lyrics and music to Nolan's songs, but comments by many people who knew him.

to this claim, Kenneth J. Bindas reports that there is "no record of his formal attendance at the school."[8]

Nolan moved to Santa Monica, California, after the 1929 stock market crash. From 1929 until 1931 he worked for a Chautauqua tent show and as a lifeguard on the beach.[9] In 1931 he answered an ad for a vocalist, "a yodeler, tenor preferred," where he met Leonard Slye (later known as Roy Rogers). Along with Bill Nichols they were a trio for the Royal Mountaineers. The trio did not have its own name at this time.[10]

When The Mountaineers failed, Nolan took a job as a caddy at Bel Air Country Club. It was while he had this job that he wrote "Tumbling Leaves," later "Tumbling Tumbleweeds." Bad weather one day kept Nolan in his apartment, and from his window he watched leaves blown by the wind tumble down the street. The poem he wrote that day later became the song.

In 1933, Leonard Slye, Tim Spencer, and Nolan formed a group called the Pioneer Trio and soon got a radio show of their own. In 1934, Harry Hall said on the air that they were too young to be Pioneers and called them "Sons of the Pioneers." The name stuck, and the most famous and long-lived Western singing group was born.

With the rapid increase of their popularity, more pressure was placed on Nolan to write new songs. He did not follow the typical cowboy song pattern of thirty-two bars. His music was different. "We wasn't going to do anything that anybody else did at all," Nolan would say many years later.[11] Kenneth Bindas adds considerably more to Nolan's claim. He points out the greater complexity about the Western cowboy in Nolan's songs:

> His songs moved toward a more sophisticated theme as he emphasized the value of the individual searching in nature for an explanation of "why we are here." His songs do not simply detail the battle between good and bad men. Instead they are concerned with the separation of truth from illusion. During the wanderlust, the hero endures the deprivations of loneliness in order to achieve understanding. The isolation causes self-examination, and Nolan's

8. Bindas, "Western Mystic," 443.

9. Griffis, *Hear My Song*, 134.

10. Ibid. Elizabeth MacDonald points out that the trio did not have a name in the Mountaineers.

11. Douglas Green Interview, www/bobnolan-sop.net, June 20, 2008.

Western man is uplifted by the discovery of the truth that exists within himself and is called forth by nature.[12]

In 1935, The Sons of the Pioneers entered the movies, where Nolan's music would gain its greatest popular attention. Appearing first with Gene Autry, then with Charles Starrett through 1940, the Sons of the Pioneers were invited to join old friend Roy Rogers in 1941 to do a singing cowboy film at Republic Studios. This began a long and fruitful relationship between Rogers and the Sons.

Between 1935 and 1949, Nolan and the Pioneers performed more than sixty-nine of Nolan's songs in more than seventy films.[13] In the thirties, forties, and fifties, Nolan wrote more than 1500 songs. By the end of his life he had more than 2000.[14]

Nolan left the Sons of the Pioneers in 1949, and, while he made subsequent recordings with them until 1958, he basically retired. In 1942 Nolan had married Clara "Peanuts" Nolan. Later the two of them would enjoy his long retirement, going back and forth between their home in the Fernando Valley and their place near Big Bear Lake. During retirement Nolan was considered a recluse by some in the entertainment field, but Elizabeth MacDonald reports that Nolan and his spouse had "a circle of good friends, including some of the Sons of the Pioneers and their families." MacDonald maintains that it was "because he didn't socialize with the Hollywood/Western Music group he'd been a part of for so long," that "*those* people considered him a recluse."[15] He died of a heart attack on June 16, 1980. His ashes were spread across the Nevada desert as he had instructed in his poem, "My Mistress: The Desert": his ashes should be scattered "in a long, straight line" so that his mistress, the desert, could find him there.[16]

Nolan's Religious Views

Nolan's songs "Cool Water" and "Tumbling Tumbleweeds" intimate things spiritual or use nature or human desire and striving against the

12. Bindas, "Western Mystic," 449.

13. Ibid., 446.

14. Green Interview.

15. MacDonald email, June 23, 2008.

16. See O'Neal and Goodwin, *Sons of the Pioneers*, 205.

background of some ultimate reality. Desert and prairie have a metaphoric reference to some more encompassing fulfillment.

Yet it is difficult to get a bead on Nolan's religious views. For one thing, he was a very private person and a loner to boot. Snuff Garret reports a comment made to him by Roy Rogers: "Snuff, I've known you about 15 years. I've known Bob Nolan for close to 50 years, and I know you a hell of a lot better than I'll ever know Bob Nolan."[17]

It is not surprising, then, that except in his songs, he did not say much, at least publicly, about things religious. What he did say is fragmentary and not explained. I cannot develop his religious views in terms of the full range of his songs in the space allocated here. I shall confine my remarks in this paper largely to "Cool Water" and "Tumbling Tumbleweeds." I only regret that I cannot give attention to the beautiful melodies of these two songs, which, perhaps, move well beyond the claims of the words themselves.

With this said, it is quite clear that Nolan's religious views were not conventional. According to Ken Griffis, he wrote very few religious songs, and, while he took pride in them, "he was at odds with established religion."[18] Nolan especially had "a strong distaste" for the tenets of established religion, feeling that so much of church teaching was "foolish talk." Yet he did think that "some power established the universe." According to Griffis, who knew him better than most, Nolan viewed his religious songs as "a sellout" in the sense that they did not represent his real concept of God. Rather, Griffis states that Nolan read Spinoza and that Nolan's point of view was closer to that of the seventeenth-century philosopher.[19]

---

17. Snuff Garret, Web Interview, www/bobnolan-sop.net, June 20, 2008.

18. Griffis, *Hear My Song*, 135. I wonder here if Nolan's song "Lighthouse of the Lord" would not fall into this category of a song that does not fit Nolan's view of God. In the lyrics the cross stands as a lighthouse still burning. It is a lighthouse where there needs to be no fear, indeed, where one can hear a mighty voice that rolls the tempest away and where we find the hands bearing the nail marks of Calvary, and calls us to come safely home.

19. Griffis, Interview. I find no evidence that Nolan was reading Spinoza in his teens and twenties, especially if he were never formally a student at the University of Arizona. Elizabeth MacDonald confirms my surmise that "His ideas or convictions were formed before he read the philosophers, although he did delve into them after retirement." MacDonald email, June 23, 2008. Nevertheless, one could do an interesting interpretation of both "Cool Water" and "Tumbling Tumbleweeds" using Spinoza's view of God and analyzing them in terms of substance, attribute, mode, thought, and extension. See John Wild, ed., *Spinoza Selections* (New York: Scribner, 1930) 45–93.

Perhaps we can look at Nolan's more mature views by examining briefly his song "The Relative Man," which was included in a Jim Nabor's album entitled "I See God," and his poem "My Mistress." "The Relative Man" was a song Snuff Garrett selected from a box of Nolan's lyrics for Nabors, a friend of Snuff's, to use in his album. Elizabeth MacDonald reports that after Nolan retired, he refused to write songs on demand. He wrote them for himself, while hoping that someone might use them in recordings.[20]

About "The Relative Man" Nolan states:

[I]t was the first time I ever deviated from the Bible teachings and more or less wrote from my own feelings, see, in the religious style. Because, you know, songs I have written in the religious vein are strictly . . . I mean, anybody can apply it to any religion—what I say in my songs—to theirs. I don't try to make any waves at all but on this one I did deviate a little bit . . . .[21]

The song is the story of a friend who in a vision confronts an ongoing range of mountains that runs infinitely into the distance. A voice tells the friend that he is a part of this vast expanse of a universe that is relative to God as God is relative to him. The friend is told that some day a bit of him will just go away, but that the much greater and most precious part, that part that is indestructible, will be carried in a mist into the farthest distances of heaven, there to reside until he shall be returned to the earth. Then in ways without number he will be connected with, indeed, be a part of the earth and relative to it forever.

The poem, "My Mistress: The Desert," suggests that the desert Nolan once knew may be gone, but he does not believe it.[22] Rather the desert has just grown cold. He plans to return to the desert and has already told the pilot who will fly his ashes to their final destination there "to scatter them in a long straight line." His mistress will then greet him gently and warmly saying that he is now finally and forever home. Shaking loose wildflowers bound up in her hair, she will then cover them both, making them warm again everlastingly in the desert.

20. MacDonald email, June 23, 2008.

21. Green Interview. The lyrics of "The Relative Man" can be seen on the website www/bobnolan-sop.net, June 20, 2008.

22. For the text of "My Mistress" see the website, www/bobnolan-sop.net.

In both the song and the poem, Nolan's profound love of nature and the world come through. The earth exists forever, and the desert becomes the place that is ultimately and finally home where the most precious part of him will last forever as part of the earth, connected with and relative to everything else. In the poem the scene becomes heavily personified with the desert now becoming a mistress who welcomes him and covers them both with wildflowers from her hair.

In both the song and the poem, ultimate destiny is a union of Nolan and nature, more specifically of Nolan and the desert, with the latter as home. Except for his mistress, the desert, no one else is mentioned. It is finally a home with him and the flower-strewn desert. The individualism seems ultimate; the isolation from others seems unrelieved with no need for others. Reunion with the earth is enough. Perhaps Nolan understands that others participate in this same coming home, but they are not mentioned.

If this poem and song represent the mature view of Nolan, we can now examine "Cool Water" and "Tumbling Tumbleweeds" as "works on the way." It must be kept in mind, however, that according to Nolan himself he never accepted established religion and its tenets. So I will try not to give these two songs a reading that ignores these claims from Nolan himself.

"Cool Water"

With Nolan's song "Cool Water" I am never sure where his language is about the desert and where it is about the entire world as a place of illusion. Surely it is about the desert, but it opens the door to contemplation of the world as such. Writing "Cool Water" out of his (Nolan's) inspiration from the desert, Griffis states that Nolan remarked many times his surprise that people think the song is about water. In Nolan's mind the song is about the absence of water. There is no water; water is an illusion.[23]

So, then, when one reads, "All day I face the barren waste without the taste of water," the absence of water is clearly named. The words "all day" can convey not only one day but all days. This line can also speak to the destitution of unemployed selves in empty careers, or those who live out dead marriages in unholy pretension, or those with the amputations

---

23. Griffis, www/bobnolan-sop.net.

of grief when loss scalds the best moments of memory, or those without aim who limp toward death in retirement, or those who live in suffocating oppression trying to get through the day, to name only a few. So the barren absence of "water" cannot be limited to the Southwest desert alone or to one day.

All the more difficult then is Nolan's reported claim that there is no water, that it is illusion. Some say Dan is a mule, others a horse, but both Dan and Nolan move with desert-burnt throats and souls crying for water. The ensoulment of the mule or horse makes this parched thirst even more pervasive. While throats are burned dry in the search for water, souls also cry out, suggesting that it is more than a physical need alone. Human and animal are caught not only with a physical need for water, but with a craving, unquenchable desire for some assuagement to slake the arid unmet claims of life itself.

The chorus becomes strange, indeed, if this thirst cannot be met. Nolan alerts Dan to keep moving and not to listen to a "devil of a man" who scatters illusions of water across the barren desert. If there is finally no water, why does Nolan instruct Dan not to listen to this demon but to keep moving? A claim can be made that moving on is all one can do. But that's not true; one can just lie down and die. Instead, in the second half of the chorus Nolan uses vision to keep Dan and himself moving. The lyric asks Dan if he can see a "big green tree" where there is real water that is running free and waiting their arrival. Nothing in the lyric suggests that that big green tree is actually there—at least not visibly so. The appeal seems to be for Dan to use his imagination, his vision.

The big green tree can be simply a sign of oasis, of water. Or, is this the tree of life? Is this the representation of fertility, of sustained life, of immortality or eternal life? We do not know, but the vision offers water that is running free. This sense of an abundance, of being uncontained, of running without limitation, unlike the barren wasteland spread with illusion. More than that, the water is waiting for Dan and for Nolan. It seems placed there for them, anticipating them.

The second verse extends this thirst beyond the heat of the day. While the nights are cool, they continue with illusion. Each star becomes "a pool of water." If the desert heat gives way to cool nights, the propensity for illusion continues, so that now making it through the day is followed by the necessity of making it through the night. But with the dawn, one only wakes and yawns and begins again the quest for water.

The incessant search for water continues day and night, seeming to suggest it is forever.

In the third verse we find shadows that sway and at least "seem" to pray for water. This personification of nature, or at least, of shadows praying offers some sense that all of nature, even shadows, join in this incessant search for water that is not there. The very notion that shadows pray provides not only an abjectly arid scene but a desiccated world.

Then, in that same verse we find an affirmation that "way up there" God will answer these prayers and disclose the location of water. This suggests that God is a long distance from this waterless world. One can certainly read this as a deity completely beyond the desert of human desire. This God does not bring us water, but rather will show us where it is.

In the fourth verse the lyric says that Dan's feet are sore and that he is yearning for one thing more than only water. He is yearning for rest, but it is not only rest. It is a rest from the quest for water. The claim that Dan's feet are sore is a striking introduction to this verse. The juxtaposition of sore feet with a craving to end all yearning provides, on the one hand, a concrete every day expression of physical weariness but, on the other, it is an exhausted fatigue with desire itself. It seems to be the desire to end all stimulation in a world devoid of cool, clear water. Such a claim would clearly be the wish for death, not only an end to all striving, but an end to stimulation itself, a desire to end all desire. This is not Augustine's notion that all our desires find their aim in God and hence completion and fulfillment. But rather this strikes an end to the hope of fulfillment as well as the very search for water itself.

Yet, still, each of these verses is followed with the chorus warning Dan of the illusions spread upon the desert, but then calling him to envision a big green tree where there is abundant water that runs freely and awaits the two of them.

There is more complexity in this song than I thought those first few hundred times I heard it early in my life. I now read it and sing it as a description of the world: the torrid absence of water in a desert filled with illusions. The night as the day is filled with deceptions. The search for elusive satisfaction is pervasive and almost endless. The craving for "cool, clear water" is found in animals that have souls and imaginations. In this world even shadows seem to pray for water, so that all of nature seems surrendered to a craving bedeviled by illusion. The hope seems to be in a far away God who can, nevertheless, lead us to a big green tree where there is no end of water.

Tumbling Tumbleweeds

The song "Tumbling Tumbleweeds" expands this picture even further insofar as it introduces a freedom found in the loneliness of wandering with the tumbleweeds. The better known lyric that begins with "a roaming cowboy" was not written by Nolan, but by later editors. His original verses begin with the claim that, while he confronts dreary days, he is not wearied by them. There is no mention of the "tumbleweeds singing" a lonely tune. No consolation is needed for his heart. With each dawn he is out "rolling with the tumbling tumbleweeds."

The chorus follows immediately, suggesting that the chorus is the tune he sings. If so, the song is about tumbleweeds that roll along and pledge "their love to the ground." This striking line conveys more than merely staying on the surface of the earth; this is a commitment to the range, a commitment shared by Nolan because he, too, will continue to be found there, "lonely but free" and drifting as the tumbleweeds do. Here freedom seems to be associated with roaming, wandering, a kind of aimlessness, blown about as the tumbleweeds are.

In the next verse, we learn that past cares are left behind, while Nolan has no end for his journey save that of following only where the trail winds, moving with the tumbleweeds wherever they go. This is the only suggestion of a trail in the entire song, but still it is a trail following the tumbleweeds. This is a strange freedom simply to follow tumbleweeds and to go wherever they lead.

The third verse is simply stunning. It is an outright affirmation of faith that when the night is over, a new world will be "born at dawn." With this line the night takes on a new meaning. While the night is lonely and the place where Nolan sings his song, it seems to be more than that. It is superseded; it is followed by dawn and issues in a new world. Then the very next line asserts that Nolan will "keep rolling along" with a song deep in his heart. It is here on the range that Nolan belongs, still drifting with the tumbling tumbleweeds.

It is not clear here whether Nolan's continuing to roll along is in the world we have now with each morning's new dawn, or if this new dawn is yet to come. I think it is both. On the one hand, he continues to roll along, but now with this confidence in a new dawn in the day-to-day world. On the other hand, when that new world comes, he continues to roll along in a new expression of freedom. Still, in the new world he continues to roll with the tumbleweeds. The new dawn is not an escape from the range, but the completion of it. It is the creation of a new range.

Verse four now gives to the chorus an ultimacy it has not had before. The context has now changed. The tumbling tumbleweeds now pledge "their love to the ground" in the sense that the tumbleweeds and the ground now participate in a new dawn. I do find it strange, however, even with Nolan's widespread reputation for being a loner, that he remains "lonely but free" in this new dawn. This new dawn seems to provide a union for Nolan and the tumbleweeds and freedom, but not with anyone else. Or, do I make too much of the chorus following verse four? Has Nolan returned here to the range as we know it? Has he moved back to the world as it is, still awaiting the new dawn?

"Tumbling Tumbleweeds" has Nolan's sensibility that nature is alive. Tumbleweeds sing, and they lead Nolan by their random tumbling to freedom where one abandons the cares of the past. It is a lonely freedom, but the tumbleweeds provide the trail, a trail it seems that will only be known at its end, not ahead of time or as it occurs. The only assurances are that freedom lies in following the tumbleweeds and that a new world will be born at dawn.

Conclusion

In "Cool Water" the issue is an unquenchable thirst that is constantly tempted by illusion. All the universe seems to be under the falsification of such mirages. In "Tumbling Tumbleweeds" the issue is freedom, a lonely freedom found only in the wandering that follows the random trails of the tumbleweeds. In "Cool Water" the answer is in the vision of a big green tree that provides abundant, free-flowing satisfaction with a God who will lead one to it. In "Tumbleweeds" the answer is found in the dawning of a new world where one does not leave the range, but finds there the place where one finally belongs. The two songs together join an insatiable yearning for the slaking of thirst while the other offers a wandering that seems to constitute freedom itself.

As noted above, "Cool Water" and "Tumbling Tumbleweeds" come early in Nolan's career, but there is a connection between these two songs and the later works of "Relative Man" and "My Mistress—The Desert." For all the desire to drink deeply of life without illusion in "Cool Water" and to fulfill freedom in lonely wandering in "Tumbleweeds," it is the desert and the lonely range that are the site of a final satisfaction of yearning and the completion of freedom. It is the earth, not some distant heaven removed from it where fulfillment of all things occurs.

These two songs presage his later views in "Relative Man" and "My Mistress." In the former, home is finally on the earth where one's most precious substance is ultimately brought back, a return captured in the latter by the re-embrace by his paramour who covers him in wildflowers.

As a Christian, I quarrel with Nolan about the necessity of freedom, as such, being so private and lonely. I question an individualism that seems implicit and pervasive in his work. I wonder why the desert is a mistress, and why there is not a party, at least with the Sons of the Pioneers and many, many others. It is not enough for the desert to be warm, even with flowers; it must also break forth into joy.

But I am profoundly instructed by his description of a world where deceits and delusions fill our minds and corrupt the desires of our lives so that our hungers are misplaced and our strivings are futile. I delight in his love for the earth and its vitalities and for his sensibilities that the new dawn and the great green tree are not abstracted from desert and prairie, but participate in a new creation that includes both. And, of course, I am grateful that he could place such things in melodies that betray his lonely world and give us such beautiful hints of a completion that even he and certainly all the rest of us cannot imagine.

Witnessing Women:
The Ministry of Women in Early Methodism

Cindy Wesley

> . . . she strove to cast her mite into the sacred treasury, by meeting classes, holding meetings for prayer, visiting the sick, by epistolary correspondence, and spiritual conversation when in company with others . . .[1]

Introduction

In the eighteenth century, an evangelical revival of religion reshaped Christianity in Great Britain. The Wesleyan Methodist branch of this revival awakened the souls of many people, but Methodism's largest listening and participating audience consisted of women. Women made up over half of the membership of the Methodist societies. A study of the Bristol societies in 1783 revealed that there were two female converts for every male.[2] Likewise, at the end of the eighteenth century, 56 percent of the 500 Methodists in the Macclesfield area were women, half of those being unmarried.[3] While the numbers of women in Methodist societies were not unlike those in the Church of England, the scope of involvement went beyond the traditional roles for females in the Anglican Church.[4] Methodist women were responsible for their spiritual development as

1. John Pipe, "Account of Miss Isabella Wilson, *Arminian Magazine* (1808) 372.

2. David Bebbington, *Evangelicalism in Modern Britain* (London: Unwin Hyman, 1989) 26.

3. David Hempton, *Methodism and Politics in British Society 1750–1850* (London: Hutchinson, 1984) 13.

4. Earl Kent Brown, *Women of Mr. Wesley's Methodism* (Lewiston: Edwin Mellen, 1983) 3–4.

they participated in a community that guided the piety of its members. The movement afforded women significant leadership roles. They founded Methodist societies, day schools, and the first Sunday schools. Women led Methodist classes and bands, visited the sick and imprisoned, and held many male preachers in the Methodist Connexion accountable for the content of their sermons and their personal conduct.

John Wesley encouraged the spiritual development of women in the Methodist movement. Wesley corresponded with numerous women who became significant leaders among the Methodists. A few of these became his close confidantes; he referred to them as his "Sisters." Wesley held women responsible for the discipline and development of their souls and demanded from them a high level of self-examination and piety that bore fruit in their outward actions. He expected the work of the Holy Spirit in their lives to be evident in their leadership and service. Indeed, he assumed that women would minister to others as a natural outgrowth of the inward conversion they had experienced. Wesley encouraged his "Sisters" to embrace their gifts for spiritual conversation and testimony, which they exercised in both private and public spheres. Eventually, he had to move from being a mentor and supporter of women's leadership to becoming a defender of their ability to witness and exhort publicly.

Wesley's Correspondence

The content of Wesley's letters demonstrates his belief that women could reach the pinnacle of spiritual growth in sanctification and perfect Christian love. First, however, they had to receive justification by understanding and accepting the free gift of God's grace. He often persuaded his female acquaintances to believe in Jesus Christ. In February, 1758, Wesley told Dorothy Furly to accept the freeness of God's gift because God was ready to give her pardon, through the advocacy of Jesus Christ.[5] Similarly, in response to Elizabeth Hardy's concern for her soul, he wrote, "He died for your sins; and he is now pleading for you at the right hand of God. O look unto him and be saved! He loves you freely, without any merit of yours. He has atoned for all your sins."[6] Several of Wesley's fe-

5. John Wesley, *The Letters of John Wesley*, ed. John Telford (London: Epworth, 1960) 4:5.

6. Ibid., 20.

male friends, including Hannah Ball and Sarah Ryan, credited him with bringing them into a state of concern for their souls.

When one of Wesley's correspondents was striving for a higher gift of grace, he might encourage her to move forward through intense self-reflection. In letters to his closest confidants, Wesley asked probing questions about their spiritual lives. Often his questions were direct and demanded intense self-analysis. For example, Wesley asked Miss March, a wealthy Methodist band leader, if her heart was still whole with God, if she sought happiness only in God, if she was sensible in God's presence, and if she found communion with God.[7] In February 1758, he enquired of Sarah Ryan, "I know you gave up the whole to God at once; but do you stand to the gift?"[8] He went on to ask if her soul was still "swallowed up in God's."[9] In April 1764, Wesley questioned Ryan's sense of assurance by asking if she found a "direct witness" that she was saved from sin, if she had evidence of eternal things that was as clear and strong as evidence of temporal things, if she ever experienced a lowness of spirit, and if she ever found her thoughts wandering.[10] His questions were intended to further his friends' growth in grace and understanding. Wesley once wrote to Ryan that he wanted her understanding to be a lamp light, her words to be full of grace, and her work to bear the stamp of God.[11]

When one of his "Sisters" believed she had been sanctified, he urged her to be steadfast in her faith and hold on to her confidence. He wrote along these lines to Sarah Crosby in January, 1770:

> Nothing is more certain than that God is willing to give always what He gives once. If . . . He now gives you power to yield Him your whole heart, you may confidently expect the continuance of that power till your spirit returns to God, provided you continue watching unto prayer, denying yourself, and taking up your cross daily.[12]

The correspondence of Wesley with his "Sisters," reveals the mutual trust and respect that characterized his relationships with these women.

7. Ibid., 310.
8. Ibid., 7.
9. Ibid.
10. Ibid., 239–40.
11. Ibid., 9.
12. *Letters*, 5:171.

Although they looked to him as a spiritual father, he also accepted their criticism. This was quite remarkable considering Wesley's rather autocratic personality. The male Assistants who disagreed with him often had to rethink their positions or leave the Connexion. Sarah Ryan freely shared with Wesley the rumor that he remained friends only with those who praised him. He responded by pointing to his friendship with Mary Bosanquet and Sarah Crosby, two women who often told him when he was wrong.[13] Ryan, Bosanquet, and Crosby regularly asked about the state of Wesley's soul and encouraged him to continue preaching free grace. The letters also reveal the expectations he had of their growth and his respect for the leadership they offered. Individuals who were justified or sanctified were to share their experiences and do good works for others at every opportunity.

Holy Conversation and Correspondence

One way for Methodist women to share their experiences and exercise spiritual leadership was in their personal relationships with family, friends and correspondents. Following Wesley's own pattern and sometimes imitating his language, they engaged in holy conversation and correspondence to encourage others. Hannah Ball of High Wycombe was talented at writing letters of spiritual support and questioning. Her letters provide an interesting example because they imitate the style and purposes of Wesley's letters. Ball wrote regularly to her cousin, Miss Bedford, exhorting her to seek justification:

> Would to God that you might be saved from sin and your heart made the temple of the Holy Ghost. In vain do we think to be saved eternally, if we are not saved from sin . . . We cannot expect to be holy unless we are justified; and if we are fully convinced of the necessity thereof, we shall not rest until God speak peace to our souls . . . O, my dear cousin, seek holiness of heart and life, and then the promises of the Gospel are yours.[14]

In other letters, Ball explained and defended the teachings of the Methodists against her cousin's objections.

---

13. *Letters*, 4:233.

14. John Parker, *Memoir of Miss Hannah Ball of High Wycombe, in Buckinghamshire with Extracts from her Diary and Correspondence* (London: John Mason, 1839) 73.

Ball also wrote letters to pious friends, holding them accountable and asking for their help. In August 1769 she wrote to Mrs. Stonehill:

> I trust your mind is engaged in the work of the Lord, counting that time mis-spent which is not employed in his service. I have learnt from experience that visiting my Christian friends is a great assistance in keeping the soul alive to God, and of increasing love towards one another. When you write, exhort me to press onward; for I need being called upon, as the Lord did Moses, to speak to the children of Israel, to go forward; there being no resting place for us in this vale of tears.[15]

In letters to friends who were striving for Christian perfection, Wesley would often ask if his correspondent had a "clear witness" of being saved from sin. In a similar fashion, Ball wrote to Ann Bolton, the cornerstone of the Witney society and an unofficial Methodist itinerant preacher, in 1770 saying, "I should be exceedingly glad to hear whether you have a clear witness that you are born of God. If not, never let Him go until He blesses you . . . be assured you cannot seek in vain."[16] The correspondence between Ball and Bolton is one example of a friendship that began at the request of Wesley, who in several letters to both women expressed sadness that they were not acquainted. He believed they would benefit from friendship with one another.

Methodists were generally cautioned against engaging in frivolous speech. When they spoke, they were to engage others in spiritually edifying conversation. Women, no less than men, were expected to direct the spiritual growth of others by privately sharing their own testimony in holy conversation. The biographer of Ann Cutler wrote that the few words Cutler spoke in conversation were "seasoned with grace" and that for all her success as a leader of revivals, ". . . her greatest gift was neither argument nor exhortation in public. She had an uncommon sight into the people's states either in leading class or in private."[17]

Women served as counselors for those seeking to understand justification and Christian perfection. Elizabeth Bennis, an eminent figure of Irish Methodism, wrote to John Wesley in March 1772 requesting his

15. Ibid., 32.

16. Ibid., 68.

17. William Bramwell, *A Short Account of the Life and Death of Ann Cutler* (Sheffield: John Smith, 1839) 16–17.

advice about her relationship with Mrs. Dawson. Bennis was sharing her own testimony with Dawson to help her understand the need for justification. Wesley advised her to tell Mrs. Dawson about the promise of Christian salvation and lend her a copy of his book *A Plain Account of Christian Perfection* because the work would encourage her.[18] Frances Mortimer found comfort in her conversations with Sarah Crosby: "I met Mrs. Crosby, an eminently pious woman, of Leeds . . . She seemed much interested in my welfare, and gave me many instructions, and advised me particularly to pray with simplicity, and to request the Lord to teach me to come to him with all the simplicity of a little child."[19] Later, Mortimer was influenced by her relationship with Elizabeth Richie. After hearing Ritchie testify in a small meeting of women, she wrote, "The image of God, formed in her soul, seemed to shine forth in her prayer and conversation with people . . . She excels in pressing the people to look for higher degrees of grace."[20]

Holy conversation was an important element in class and band meetings where women took a formal role as mentors. In correspondence with female band and class leaders, Wesley offered instructions that characterized his expectations of anyone who held that office. For example, Wesley told Miss March of Bristol to hold her band members accountable. If a band member became a backslider, it was March's responsibility to discover the reason for the backsliding and exhort the member to repent. She was to encourage the more earnest of her members to strive for perfection.[21] Wesley advised Grace Walton that when leading a class meeting she should speak for four or five minutes on the proposed question for the evening and include a short exhortation.[22] The presence of female band and class leaders in early Methodism is well documented. It is still interesting, however, that Wesley himself directly instructed and supported the women who filled these leadership positions, entrusting them with the responsibility of exhorting, admonishing, and advising the souls in their care. Given Wesley's clear support of women's informal and formal leadership in the movement, it should not be surprising that many

18. Wesley, *Letters*, 5:314–15.

19. Joseph Sutcliffe, *The Experience of the Late Mrs. Frances Pawson* (London: The Conference Office, 1813) 27

20. Ibid., 51.

21. Wesley, *Letters*, 4:181.

22. Ibid., 164.

women became role models for the members of their Methodist societies
and eventually embraced a public form of ministry.

Witnessing and Preaching

In several cases, leadership of a class or a band led women to become
exhorters, itinerants, and revivalists. On February 8, 1761, Sarah Crosby,
a class leader in Leeds, wrote in her journal:

> In the evening I expected to meet about thirty persons in class:
> but to my great surprise there came near two hundred . . . I was
> not sure it was right for me to exhort in so public a manner, yet I
> saw it impracticable to meet all these people by way of speaking
> particularly to each individual. I, therefore, gave out a hymn, and
> prayed, and told them part of what the Lord had done for myself,
> persuading them to flee from all sin.[23]

Crosby was quite concerned about having spoken in such a public manner. The event caused a dilemma for Wesley because the Methodists,
despite their claims of being loyal Church members, had several ir-
regular practices. They held meetings that were outside the control of
both Church leadership and parish priests. In addition, they employed
lay preachers who were loyal and answerable only to Wesley. Allowing
women to be preachers could offend non-Methodists and Methodists
alike. In response to Crosby's experience, Wesley wrote on February 14 to
assure her that she had acted appropriately. At the same time, he advised
Crosby to approach such situations in a manner that would avoid offense
and questions of propriety by telling her audience, "You lay me under
great difficulty. The Methodists do not allow women preachers; neither
do I take upon me any such character. But I will nakedly tell what is in
my heart."[24] By the time Wesley wrote to Crosby, she had come to terms
with her new role as a public speaker. On February 13, she again spoke to
nearly two hundred people, telling them to repent and showing them the
willingness of Christ to save. She later wrote in her journal, "My soul was
much comforted in speaking to the people, as my Lord has removed all

---

23. E[lizabeth] M[ortimer], "The Grace of God Manifested in an Account of Mrs.
Crosby of Leeds," *Arminian Magazine* (1806) 518.

24. Wesley, *Letters*, 4:133.

my scruples, respecting the propriety of my acting thus publickly [sic.]."[25]
Crosby did not receive Wesley's reassuring letter until several more days
had elapsed.

According to Methodist historian Frank Baker, "There seems little
reasonable doubt that Mrs. Sarah Crosby was the first authorized woman
preacher of Methodism."[26] Crosby became an itinerant, and preached for
twenty years around Leeds. Though never assigned to a circuit, she kept
a pace similar to that of an Assistant. In 1777, Crosby wrote 166 letters,
rode 960 miles, and kept 220 public meetings and 600 private meetings.[27]
She eventually settled in Leeds with Ann Tripp, where they headed a
group of women preacher known as "The Female Brethren."[28]

Another woman who assumed leadership in a public meeting was
Ann Gilbert. She developed skills as a speaker through her leadership
of a class. However, her first opportunity to exhort in public came when
she attended a preaching meeting held in a neighboring village. When
the preacher did not come, Gilbert took charge of the meeting. She recounted the incident for *Arminian Magazine* (1795):

> In the year 1771, going one day to preaching in the adjoining vil-
> lage, the preacher happened not to come; I therefore gave out a
> hymn and went to prayer, according to my usual custom; I then
> told the people they need not be disappointed, for the Lord was
> present to bless them. Immediately I received such a manifesta-
> tion of the love and power of God, that I was constrained to in-
> treat [sic] and beseech them to repent, and turn to the Lord. All
> the people were melted into tears, and many were convinced of
> sin.[29]

Like Crosby, Ann Gilbert found 'comfort' in exhorting a congregation.
Experiencing the love and power of God while speaking was important,
not only because it gave the woman exhorter a sense of reassurance, but
also because it helped her justify her actions.

Wesley's journal entries indicate that women preachers or exhorters
became the leaders of religious revivals. In October 1779, he visited a

25. M[ortimer], "Account of Mrs. Crosby," 518.

26. Frank Baker, "John Wesley and Sarah Crosby," *Proceedings of the Wesley Historical Society* 27 (1949) 76.

27. Ibid., 79.

28. Ibid., 81.

29. Ann Gilbert, "Experiences of Mrs. Ann Gilbert," *Arminian Magazine* (1795) 44.

community where the people experienced a spiritual change because of the work of a woman. Wesley wrote, "The people here had been remarkably dead for many years; but since that saint of God, Bathsheba Hall, with her husband, came among them, a flame is broke out. The people flock together in troops, and are athirst for all the promises of God."[30]

One of Wesley's correspondents, Ann Cutler, became famous in Yorkshire and Lancashire as a revivalist. It was reported that she never preached a formal sermon using a text and exposition; instead, she simply discussed with her audiences the sinner's need of repentance.[31] She was given the nickname "Praying Nanny," which indicated the distinctive nature of her work.[32] Like Sarah Crosby and Ann Gilbert, Cutler's speaking experience began in the Methodist meetinghouse. According to her biographer and personal friend, William Bramwell, "She began to pray in meetings, and several were awakened and brought to God. The effects of her labour were manifest. Many were displeased, but some were saved."[33]

While she was a popular figure, critical remarks were made about her method of prayer because she used a "great exertion of voice."[34] Cutler realized that her manner of speaking was unusual and not to every listener's liking. In fact, Wesley advised her not to speak loudly or harshly when addressing a congregation. She did not change her style because it gave her strength to continue her work. In defending herself she claimed, "I have tried to pray differently, but I am always less confident. I would do anything to please if it would not hurt my own soul: but I am in this way the most free from wanderings, and have the greatest confidence. I dare not strive against it any more."[35]

Despite her style of speaking, Cutler was an effective revivalist who could sway an entire congregation. William Bramwell itinerated with her and witnessed the effect she had on a crowd. He wrote in Cutler's biography, "I have been in chapel when suddenly the whole congregation had

---

30. John Wesley, *Journal*, vol. 4 of *The Works of John Wesley* (Grand Rapids: Baker, 1979) 167.

31. Leslie Church, *More about the Early Methodist People* (London: Epworth, 1949) 155.

32. Deborah Valenze, *Prophetic Sons and Daughters* (Princeton: Princeton University Press, 1985) 53, 55.

33. Bramwell, *Ann Cutler*, 6–7.

34. Ibid., 13–14.

35. Ibid.

been deeply affected in answer to her cries. For prayer, I never expect to see her equal again."[36] Although Bramwell initially tried to dissuade her from becoming an itinerant, her concern for the souls of others drove her to continue. She witnessed to the people of Otley, Oldham, Manchester, Derby and Macclesfield. Bramwell recorded Cutler's success as a revivalist, "In several places, when preachers and others had lost their hope of a revival, she has selected a few to assist her, and, to the astonishment of many, has prevailed with God."[37]

Wesley's view of women in the preaching ministry changed over a period of years as he sought to justify the *de facto* public role of women within Methodism. He was willing to accept women leaders in Methodism as emulating the female deacons of the primitive church and he had no objection to females leading class or band meetings, conducting public prayer or overtly testifying to their faith. In fact, he expected such expressions of faith. Methodist society meetings and Love Feasts were structured to allow for spontaneous witness or prayer. Wesley recorded incidents in his journal when he had been affected by the testimony or prayer offered by a woman. On July 19, 1761, he attended the Bristol Society's first Love Feast. Wesley explained to the gathering that any man or woman was free to speak to God's glory during a Love Feast:

> Several then did speak, and not in vain: The flame ran from heart to heart, especially while one was declaring, with all simplicity, the manner wherein God, during the morning sermon . . . had set her soul at liberty.[38]

On another occasion Wesley wrote about the prayer offered by a woman during a small meeting. The prayer was not skillfully developed, but it had an effect for he wrote in his journal:

> Such a prayer I have never heard before: It was perfectly an original; odd and unconnected, made up of disjointed fragments, and yet like a flame of fire. Every sentence went through my heart, and I believe the heart of everyone present.[39]

36. Ibid.

37. Ibid., 9–10.

38. John Wesley, *Journal*, vol. 3 of *The Works of John Wesley* (Grand Rapids: Baker 1979) 68.

39. Ibid., 196.

While Wesley was very supportive of women offering public testimony and prayer in Methodist meetings, he was initially resistant to
allowing women to preach. He was, after all, a High Church Anglican
priest who had initially opposed field preaching and the employment of
lay preachers, relenting only when he realized the necessity of both for
the spread of the revival. His High Church views, along with the charges
against Methodism for its unorthodox practices, and fear of offending the
social standards of the day, made it difficult for Wesley to countenance
women preachers. By 1769, Sarah Crosby had been an itinerant preacher,
in all but official title, for eight years. Yet Wesley wrote in March 1769 to
offer advice about her approach in public speaking:

> (1) Pray in private or public as much as you can.

> (2) Even in public you may properly enough intermix *short exhor-
> tation* with prayer; but keep as far from what is called preach-
> ing as you can: therefore never take a text; never speak in a
> continued discourse without some break, about four or five
> minutes. Tell the people, "We shall have another *prayer meet-
> ing* at such a time and place."[40]

The Methodists, and especially Wesley, faced a difficult choice because
they did not want to stifle the good work that might be achieved by a
female speaker, but they were anxious about giving a woman authority
to preach.

By 1771, Wesley was coming to terms with the role of women as
preachers. Prior to this time, he made clear distinctions between the
speaking of women, which he referred to as testimony or exhortation,
and preaching, which was done by the male Assistants.[41] He justified
the public role of women on the basis of four points. The first point was
a biblical argument based on the writings and actions of St. Paul, who
made exceptions to the proscription of women speaking to congregations. Paul highly praised several women who were his helpers in ministry. In this respect Wesley also turned to the model of the deaconesses in
the New Testament, including Phoebe and Priscilla, who were permitted
to pray, teach, and speak publicly. Secondly, Wesley believed that some
women had an extraordinary call to be instruments of God's work in the
Methodist movement. In 1771, Wesley wrote to Mary Bosanquet, one of

40. Wesley, *Letters*, 5:130–31 (italics in original).
41. Brown, *Women*, 26, 28.

the female exhorters who often preached publicly until her marriage to John Fletcher:

> I think the strength of the cause rests there—on your having an *extraordinary* call. . . . It is plain to me that the whole work of God termed Methodism is an extraordinary dispensation of His providence. Therefore I do not wonder if several things occur therein which do not fall under the ordinary rules of discipline.[42]

Women could speak publicly because they were called to do so as a part of the extraordinary act of providence known as Methodism. The same argument was used to justify the employment of lay preachers.

Thirdly, the public ministry of a woman was acceptable if it resulted from her complete devotion to God. In other words, Wesley would not give even tacit approval to a woman preaching unless the woman had a high level of inward and outward piety. Fourthly, it was also important to Wesley that the female preacher be able to demonstrate the fruits of her leadership. In other words, he would defend her ability to preach if her speaking had a positive impact on the spiritual growth of those who heard her. All preachers approved by Wesley were expected to preach Methodist doctrine. If many people responded with faith when a woman preached Methodist beliefs, he saw it as evidence that God was using her to reap a great harvest of souls. Wesley personally judged each case of a woman who expressed the desire to preach on an individual basis, determining the validity of her call, the strength of her devotion to God, and the effects of her speaking.[43] He used similar criteria to judge the fitness of his male Assistants. By 1779, Mary Bosanquet could say honestly of her public speaking, ". . . I do nothing but what Mr. Wesley approves."[44]

An entry from Wesley's journal, dated December 4, 1786, provides evidence of these criteria. He records meeting the twenty-two year old preacher Sarah Mallet, whose call to preach had been overwhelming. Mallet felt an impression that she "ought to call sinners to repentance."[45] She resisted, believing that she was unqualified, and soon began falling

---

42. Wesley, *Letters*, 5:257.

43. Church, *More About*, 141.

44. Henry Moore, *The Life of Mrs. Mary Fletcher, Consort and Relict of The Rev. John Fletcher, Vicar of Madeley, Salop: Compiled from Her Journal and Other Authentic Documents* (London: 1818) 119.

45. Wesley, *Journal*, 4:356.

unconscious and imagined herself to be preaching to a large congregation. His journal entry of their encounter reads:

> She fell into a fit; and while utterly senseless, thought she was in the preaching house in Lowesoft, where she prayed and preached for near an hour, to a numerous congregation. She then opened her eyes and recovered her sense. In a year or two she had eighteen of these fits; in every one of which she imagined herself to be preaching in one or another congregation.[46]

Wesley also notes there were numerous witnesses to his account of Mallet's experiences. The occurrence of these fits did not end until she promised to exhort sinners.

There is no doubt that Wesley judged Mallet's call to be extraordinary. He also found that she had a strong understanding of the faith and was devoted to God. In October 1787, she was given authority to preach by an Assistant named Joseph Harper who claimed he had acted "by order of Mr. Wesley and the Conference."[47] Mallet became the first licensed female preacher in the Methodist Connexion.

Comparatively few women became itinerant preachers, perhaps no more than twenty-seven in Wesley's lifetime.[48] While he knew about their work, and in some instances, offered words of guidance, there was no move by the Wesleyan Connexion to give women exhorters the status of Assistants by assigning them to circuits or making small salary provisions. The eminent Methodist historian Richard Heitzenrater notes that Wesley's tight control over interviewing and determining which women were permitted to preach was a "private accommodation and did not change the normal discipline of the connection."[49] Similarly, Paul Chilcote suggests that Wesley's acceptance of certain women preachers was a compromise position. By defending the call of some extraordinary women, Wesley could lessen the prejudice against them while the movement benefited from the tremendous blessing their work yielded.[50] The

---

46. Ibid.

47. Church, *More About*, 140.

48. Brown, *Women*, 237.

49. Richard Heitzenrater, *Wesley and the People Called Methodists* (Nashville: Abingdon, 1995) 248.

50. Paul Chilcote, *John Wesley and the Women Preachers of Early Methodism* (Metuechen, NJ: Scarecrow, 1991) 171.

women continued to be assured by their faith and moments of success such as one described by Ann Cutler, whose preaching brought "near a hundred" souls to God: "I am closely united to Jesus; it is heaven below and my desire for the salvation of others is so great that I can spend and be spent for the Lord."[51]

Lasting Influence

The witness of the early Methodist women, along with Wesley's encouragement and defense of their leadership, was essential to the early Methodist movement. Women were strongly attracted to the movement. They were supported and given opportunities to be mentors and leaders; roles that Wesley believed were appropriate and biblical. After his death, however, the British Methodist Conference moved decisively in 1803 to restrict the opportunities for women to offer public exhortation outside of small group meetings.[52] The Conference rule did not prevent women from continuing in their longstanding roles as class and band leaders, or their private engagement in spiritual conversation and correspondence. Without Wesley there to defend them, however, women were not permitted to preach to mixed audiences, nor were they allowed to speak to any group outside of their local area without the permission of two superintendents.

Still, the ministry of the early Methodist women, including their preaching role, continued in the popular memory of the Methodists for at least another generation. Biographies of Wesley's "Sisters" appeared in the nineteenth century. In 1818 Henry Moore published *The Life of Mrs. Mary Fletcher, Consort and Relict of The Rev. John Fletcher, Vicar of Madeley, Salop: Compiled from Her Journal and Other Authentic Documents*, which recounted Mary Bosanquet Fletcher's tremendous involvement in the Methodist movement including founding the Leeds Society, establishing the Leytonstone school and orphanage, itinerating, and sharing ministry with her husband John Fletcher. In 1839 John Parker published *Memoir of Miss Hannah Ball of High Wycombe, in Buckinghamshire with Extracts from her Diary and Correspondence*. Ball founded a Sunday school for

---

51. Bramwell, *Ann Cutler*, 23–24.

52. Wesley Swift, "Women Itinerant Preachers of Early Methodism," *Proceedings of the Wesley Historical Society* 28 (1952) 90.

child laborers in the 1760s. The memory of her work on behalf of impoverished children is enshrined today in the Hannah Ball School, a private preschool for children of all economic backgrounds, in the village of High Wycombe. In the same year that Parker's book appeared, William Bramwell, a well-known Methodist itinerant, published A *Short Account of the Life and Death of Ann Cutler* as a tribute to "Praying Nanny," the woman who had itinerated with him.

Later in the nineteenth century, Catherine Booth, co-founder of the Salvation Army and a dynamic preacher in her own right, wrote two pamphlets in defense of women preaching and teaching in public. Her arguments relied on the memory of the Methodist women and on Wesley's support of their ministry. In both pamphlets she meticulously developed a biblical defense for women preaching, citing examples of God issuing an extraordinary call to women in texts from the Old and New Testaments.[53] She highlighted the work of the New Testament deaconess, Phoebe, who was also mentioned by Wesley in numerous letters and sermons. Booth suggested that readers should see Wesley's thoughts on Romans 16:1 in his *Notes on the New Testament.*[54] In addition to her biblical argument, Booth noted the extraordinary faithfulness and spiritual development of women who have fulfilled their calling, citing several Methodist women as examples:

> [T]here have been some in all ages in whom the Holy Ghost has wrought so mightily, that at the sacrifice of reputation and all things most dear, they have been compelled to come out as witnesses for Jesus and ambassadors of His gospel. As a rule, these women have been amongst the most devoted and self-denying of the Lord's people, giving indisputable evidence by the purity and beauty of their lives that they were led by the Spirit of God. Now, if the word of God forbids female ministry, we would ask how it happens that so many of the most devoted handmaidens of the Lord have felt themselves constrained by the Holy Ghost to exercise it . . . . Will any one venture to asset that such women as Mrs. Elizabeth Fry, Mrs. Fletcher of Madeley, and Mrs. Smith have been deceived with respect to their call to deliver the gospel message to their fellow-creatures? If not, then God does call and

53. Catherine Mumford Booth, *Female Teaching: Or, The Rev. A. A. Rees versus Mrs. Palmer, Being a Reply to a Pamphlet by the Above Gentleman on the Sunderland Revival* (London: G. J. Stephenson, 1861) 11.

54. Ibid.

qualify women to preach, and His word, rightly understood, cannot forbid what His Spirit enjoins.[55]

Booth made additional references to women who were leaders in the Methodist revival, including Hester Roe Rogers, Frances Mortimer Pawson, and Ann Cutler. She also highlighted the work of Mary Bosanquet Fletcher:

> This eminently devoted lady opened an orphan house, and devoted her time, her heart, and her fortune, to the work of the Lord. The Rev. Mr. Hodson, in referring to her public labours says, "Mrs. Fletcher was not only luminous but truly eloquent—her discourses displayed much good sense, and were fraught with the riches of the gospel. She excelled in that poetry of an orator which can alone supply the place of all the rest—that eloquence which goes directly to the heart. She was the honoured instrument of doing much good; and the fruit of her labours is now manifest in the lives and tempers of numbers who will be her crown of rejoicing in the day of the Lord.[56]

It is obvious from Booth's writings that Wesley and several significant Methodist women influenced her views on the equality of women and the right of women to preach. She exerted an influence over the development of the Salvation Army, which characteristically allowed women to have roles equal to those of men.

John Wesley constantly supported the fruitful leadership and moved to defend the public testimony of women in his movement. At the same time, he expected no less of them than Christian perfection: "I want you to live like an angel here below, or rather like the Son of God. Woman walk thou as Christ walked."[57] The women responded and were heartened in their efforts. They witnessed to the work of God's grace in their lives through private and public forms of ministry and provided lasting examples of faithfulness for the people called Methodists.

---

55. Ibid., 20.
56. Ibid., 21–22.
57. Wesley, *Letters*, 4:4–5.

Born of Conviction:
White Methodist Witness to Mississippi's Closed Society*

Joseph T. Reiff

> [I]n writing this . . . , I am wounding some of the dearest people
> in the world, but Jesus says, "He that loves father or mother more
> than Me is not worthy of Me." [1]

The second-best-known white clergy statement in the Civil Rights era,
"Born of Conviction," appeared in *The Mississippi Methodist Advocate* on
January 2, 1963, signed by twenty-eight ministers of the white Mississippi
Conference (hereafter referred to as the twenty-eight).[2] In 1963, The
Methodist Church maintained a segregated structure, so in addition to
the two white annual conferences, Mississippi and North Mississippi,
there were two black conferences—Mississippi and Upper Mississippi,
part of the larger Central Jurisdiction—in the state. The statement by the
twenty-eight was written in that context and in response to the turmoil
of early 1960s Mississippi, especially the aftermath of the September 1962
riot at Ole Miss on the day James Meredith arrived there to enroll as the
school's first African-American student. It called for freedom of the pulpit,
reminded readers of the Methodist *Discipline*'s claim that the teachings
of Jesus "[permit] no discrimination because of race, color, or creed," ex-

* This account is drawn from research for the book I am writing, *Born of Conviction:
White Methodists and Mississippi's Closed Society*, with partial support provided by a
Religious Institutions Grant, Louisville Institute; the McConnell Scholarship, Emory
& Henry College; and the Mednick Fellowship, Virginia Foundation for Independent
Colleges. The author has copies of all unpublished documents cited.

1. Antonina Canzoneri, *Mississippi Baptist Record*, November 15, 1962.

2. The best-known is the April 1963 statement issued by 11 Alabama white clergy, to
which Martin Luther King Jr. responded in the "Letter from Birmingham Jail."

pressed support for the public schools and opposition to any attempt to close them, and affirmed the signers' opposition to Communism.

Its publication caused a firestorm of controversy. Though some public affirmation of the statement came from a few lay and clergy persons, the overwhelming response was negative, including numerous expressions of shock, outrage, and hurt, along with ostracism, persecution, threats, and some violence. There was also little support from Conference leaders. Within eighteen months, eighteen of the twenty-eight had left the Mississippi Conference, and two others departed in the next few years.

The Born of Conviction story belongs in the growing literature on the roles (positive, negative, and ambivalent) that Southern white Christians played in the larger ecology of change during the Civil Rights era. This essay explores the context in which the twenty-eight felt called to make their witness, the creation of the statement and the recruiting of signers, responses to its publication, and what became of the twenty-eight, then closes with some brief reflections on the larger meaning of Born of Conviction.[3]

A Time to Speak to the "Closed Society"

The events surrounding James Meredith's admission to Ole Miss, including the refusal of many white Mississippi politicians and citizens to accept any blame for the atmosphere that resulted in violence, provided the centerpiece for Ole Miss historian James Silver's argument that the state had become a Closed Society. This Closed Society insisted on the maintenance of segregation and white supremacy and demanded "loyalty to the united front, requiring that non-conformists and dissenters

3. Examples of this "growing literature" include, on the denominational level, Peter C. Murray, *Methodists and the Crucible of Race, 1930–1975* (Columbia: University of Missouri Press, 2004); Gardiner H. Shattuck Jr., *Episcopalians and Race: Civil War to Civil Rights* (Lexington: University Press of Kentucky, 2000); Mark Newman, *Getting Right with God: Southern Baptists and Desegregation, 1945–1995* (Tuscaloosa: University of Alabama Press, 2001); and Joel L. Alvis, Jr., *Religion & Race: Southern Presbyterians, 1946-1983* (Tuscaloosa: University of Alabama Press, 1994); on the role of Jewish rabbis, see Mark K. Bauman and Berkley Kalin, editors, *The Quiet Voices: Southern Rabbis and Black Civil Rights, 1880s to 1990s* (Tuscaloosa: University of Alabama Press, 1997); on the responses of Methodists in one state or annual conference, see Donald E. Collins, *When the Church Bell Rang Racist: The Methodist Church and the Civil Rights Movement in Alabama* (Macon: Mercer University Press, 1998); and James T. Clemons and Kelly L. Farr, editors, *Crisis of Conscience: Arkansas Methodists and the Civil Rights Struggle* (Little Rock: Butler Center for Arkansas Studies, 2007).

from the code be silenced, or, in a crisis, driven from the community."
Another interpreter of the Mississippi Civil Rights era says that after the
1954 *Brown* decision most white Mississippians had "developed a siege
mentality so pervasive it encompassed virtually every citizen and institution," and "preserving the southern way of life soon assumed all the
trappings of a holy crusade." Roy C. Clark, pastor of Jackson's Capitol
Street Methodist Church from 1953–1963, summed up the situation in
this way: ". . . we were making a god of segregation, and everything else
was made subservient to it."[4]

For some Mississippi whites, the Ole Miss/Oxford riot in the fall of
1962 was a defining moment. The "Mississippi standard version" of the
riot placed the blame solely on the Kennedys and the federal government, but some who had kept silent out of fear knew that the time had
come to stand up to the massive resistance to desegregation by state government and the Citizens' Council (which virtually controlled Governor
Ross Barnett). Leaders who could not be dismissed as "radical outsiders"
needed to break the pattern of rigid conformity to the Closed Society.[5]

Some moderate leaders began to speak out. In the week after the riot,
a small ecumenical group of Oxford clergy issued a call "for repentance
for our collective and individual guilt in the formation of the atmosphere
which produced the strife at the University of Mississippi and Oxford. . . ."
A few weeks later, Mississippi Southern Baptists read an impassioned
response from Antonina Canzoneri, a Mississippi missionary in Nigeria:
"What do you expect of us? You send us out here to preach that Christ
died for all men. Then you make a travesty of our message by refusing
to associate with some of them just because of the color of their skin."
Quite aware of the cost of her words, Canzoneri added: "Ross Barnett is
my cousin, and in writing this letter, I am wounding some of the dearest

4. On the September 30 riot and the conditions that caused it, see William Doyle,
An American Insurrection: The Battle of Oxford, Mississippi, 1962 (New York: Doubleday,
2001); on the cultural background and mindset that contributed to the riot, see Paul
Hendrickson, *Sons of Mississippi: A Story of Race and Its Legacy* (New York: Vintage,
2003); James Silver, *Mississippi: The Closed Society*, new enlarged edition (New York:
Harcourt, Brace, & World, 1966) 6; John Dittmer, *Local People: The Struggle for Civil
Rights in Mississippi* (Urbana: University of Illinois Press, 1994) 58, 41; Roy C. Clark Oral
history memoir, August 2, 1965, Millsaps College Archives, John Quincy Adams Papers
F16, Box 6, 40–41.

5. The "Mississippi standard version" phrase comes from Walker Percy, "Mississippi:
The Fallen Paradise," *Signposts in a Strange Land* (New York: Farrar, Straus, and Giroux,
1991) 43.

people in the world, but Jesus says, 'He that loves father or mother more than Me is not worthy of Me.'" Turning the usual accusations of Communist influence on the Civil Rights movement on their head, she concluded, "The Communists do not need to work against the preaching of the gospel [in Africa] by Americans; you are doing it quite adequately. Wake up! Look at what is happening in the world! Be courageous; act like Christians!"[6]

White Mississippi Methodists read a letter in the *Advocate* from one of their missionaries, Dot Hubbard, a teacher in South Korea. Her statement took a more subtle and hopeful tone by sharing the fears and doubts of her Korean students who had planned to study in the U. S., but because of news stories about the reactions of Ole Miss students to Meredith were now wondering if "perhaps there will be this same display of hatred against Oriental students." Hubbard's response was that Ole Miss "I feel sure, will now show to the world the true beauty and real strength of inner Christ-like character."[7]

North Mississippi Conference minister Sam Ashmore, editor of *The Mississippi Methodist Advocate*, a weekly newspaper serving both white Mississippi annual conferences, was sixty-eight and approaching the end of his career in October 1962. He had not been known as a particularly prophetic or "liberal" minister when he took the editor's position in 1955, but the events of the ensuing years led him to speak with uncommon boldness. In "Who Is To Blame for the Rioting?," an editorial published ten days after the riot, Ashmore said the blame belonged to "all of us," because the church had allowed "pressure groups" (like the Citizens' Council) to take control and "get our citizens to distrust the Church, the United States government and the humanitarian agencies of the United Nations." Though Methodists and other Mississippians knew this was happening, "we dared not say or do anything about it[.] . . . We protested the events which ultimately lead [sic] to the rioting at Ole Miss and we were told the shed-blood was on our hands." Evidently even mild protest

6. "Call for Repentance" appeared in *Christianity Today*, October 26, 1962, 5–36, and in *New South*, March 1963; signers included Episcopal priests Duncan M. Gray Jr. and Wofford Smith. On their attempts to stop the riot, see Doyle, *An American Insurrection*, 119–20, 160–62, 168–71; on Gray's lifelong witness, see Will D. Campbell, *And Also With You: Duncan Gray and the American Dilemma* (Franklin, TN: Providence House, 1997); *Mississippi Baptist Record*, November 15, 1962.

7. *Mississippi Methodist Advocate* (hereafter abbreviated *MMA*), November 21, 1962.

against the massive resistance juggernaut was seen as betrayal of the sacred cause of white Mississippi. "Yes, the church is partly responsible for what happened at Ole Miss," Ashmore concluded, because church people failed to speak out forcefully enough and "were not true to our Christian convictions." Now, he said, "the Church will lose her life whatever she does," and the choice facing the white Mississippi Methodist Church was "whether she loses her life for Christ's sake and finds it in this hour of crisis or whether she really loses her life in pious platitudes and innocuous activity in a day which demands courageous witness."[8]

"Our Lord Jesus Christ . . . Permits No Discrimination . . ."

The *North* Mississippi Conference District Superintendents released a statement "whole-heartedly endors[ing]" the Oxford ministers' Call for Repentance, closing with these words: "We affirm the freedom of the pulpit. We have uttermost confidence in our ministers and support them in the preaching of the whole Gospel in the Spirit of Christ." This response made the silence of Bishop Marvin Franklin and the District Superintendents of the Mississippi Conference (which covered the southern half of the state) more glaring. As October 1962 wore on, some Mississippi Conference ministers became increasingly frustrated that none of their Conference's leaders were saying anything publicly to show that at least some Mississippi Conference clergy disagreed with forced segregation, white supremacy, and "massive resistance."[9]

In late October or early November, four Mississippi Conference ministers met at a fishing cabin owned by Maxie Dunnam near Richton in southeast Mississippi. Joining Dunnam were Jerry Furr, Jerry Trigg, and Jim Waits; three were pastors on the Gulf Coast, while Furr was associate pastor at Galloway Memorial, situated a block from the State Capitol in downtown Jackson. In a marathon session, the four settled on a manifesto of about 600 words with four main points:

8. Ashmore's wife, Ann Lewis Ashmore, served as an uncredited assistant over the eleven years her husband edited the *Advocate*, and she may have written or collaborated on some editorials; some believe Ann's influence partially explains Sam's willingness to speak out more forcefully in the 1960s—author's interviews with Donald Lewis (Mrs. Ashmore's nephew), February 27, 2006, and Mabel Anne Ashmore Harjes (the Ashmore's daughter), July 22, 2006; *MMA*, October 10, 1962.

9. *MMA*, October 17, 1962; Bishop Franklin presided over both conferences and was on a trip to Asia when the North Mississippi Cabinet endorsement was released; he never commented publicly on Ole Miss.

- *Freedom of the pulpit*: "The Church is the instrument of God's purpose. . . . It is ours only as stewards under His Lordship." Clearly it was not to be used simply as a tool to prop up the Closed Society, where many ministers felt severely restricted in what they could say in churches because of widespread resistance to *any* questions raised about the status quo (the Closed Society orthodoxy). "Effective practice of this steward-ship demands . . . an atmosphere for responsible belief and free expression."

- *Affirmation of faith in "the official position of The Methodist Church on race"* as found in the 1960 *Discipline* (the denomi-nation's official book of doctrine and polity). Statements quot-ed included "Our Lord Jesus Christ teaches that all men are brothers. He permits no discrimination because of race, color, or creed," and "God is Father of all people and races; . . . all men are brothers."

- *Support for public schools and opposition to their closing when desegregation comes*: "The Methodist Church is officially com-mitted to the system of public school education and we concur. We are unalterably opposed to the closing of public schools on any level or to the diversion of tax funds to the support of pri-vate or sectarian schools."

- *Affirmation of "an unflinching opposition to Communism"*: "In these conflicting times, the issues of race and Communism are frequently confused." The Closed Society rigidity meant that anyone who dissented was routinely labeled a Communist.[10]

The statement began with these words:

> "Confronted with the grave crises precipitated by racial discord within our state in recent months, and the genuine dilemma fac-ing persons of Christian conscience, we are compelled to voice publicly our convictions. Indeed, as Christian ministers and as native Mississippians, sharing the anguish of all our people, we have a particular obligation to speak."

10. None of the participants remembers the date of the fishing cabin meeting, and I have found no written evidence to pinpoint it; the four writers and others were recruiting signers for the statement by Thanksgiving (November 22) or a few days after—author's interviews with each of the four creators of the statement (all in June or July 2004, except Waits, July 21, 2003) and Rayford Woodrick, March 11, 2004; Gene Davenport and Jerry Trigg were fellow students at Vanderbilt Divinity School in the late 1950s; *MMA*, January 2, 1963; 1960 *Discipline of The Methodist Church*, Paragraphs 2026 and 2020.

The writers felt they spoke for many Mississippi Christians struggling with a "genuine dilemma" of Christian conscience. Speaking as natives of Mississippi (i.e., "We're not 'outside agitators.'"), they sought to address the "anguish" of all who were deeply troubled by what had been happening but felt powerless to do or say anything about it.

Along with the creation of the statement came deliberations on who would be asked to sign. The original four drew up a list of names that was supplemented during at least one additional meeting in Hattiesburg in mid-December, with some other signers (and some eventual non-signers) present. The list grew to fifty-five to sixty potential signers, mostly younger members of the Conference. Some committed signers agreed to recruit other potential signers. While the ages of the eventual twenty-eight who signed the document ranged from twenty-five to fifty-six, half were under thirty and two-thirds under thirty-six. Eight were in their first year or two out of seminary.[11]

At least two who originally agreed to sign changed their minds about a week before publication. Both said it was because they had expected more signatures and believed if ministers of more standing in the Conference were to sign, the statement would carry more weight. Pastors of large churches in the Conference had, in fact, not been asked to sign. At least two other ministers agreed to sign the statement, but their names were somehow not included. Those who refused to sign gave a variety of reasons, including fear that they had not been at their churches long enough to weather the crisis if their names were included. Some said the statement did not say enough (though it is not clear they would have signed if the wording had been stronger). Some signers did not believe the statement would cause much controversy.[12]

11. Details on the weeks between the statement's creation and its publication are hazy—some of the twenty-eight remembered other gatherings of some signers before publication, and one or two remembered the writing process involving more than four (but the four writers are all sure it was only four); a list of thirty-four potential signers can be found in the Jim L. Waits Papers, Pitts Theology Library Archives, Emory University, MSS 287, Box 1, Folders 2 and 3; the names of twenty-one of the eventual signers are not on this list, and I am aware of a couple of others asked to sign; not all of the people on the list were contacted.

12. Hubert Barlow to Dunnam, December 25, 1962, and Roy Eaton to Dunnam, December 24, 1962, Maxie Dunnam Private Papers. It is unclear why larger church pastors were not included as potential signers—Jim Waits says it was because they had more to lose. Perhaps the desire for secrecy affected that decision as well: given the power of some Conference leaders, the statement's creators may have feared an attempt to prevent

"Like a Bomb Exploding"[13]

"Born of the deep conviction of our souls as to what is morally right, we have been driven to seek the foundations of such convictions in the expressed witness of our Church," the twenty-eight announced to Mississippi Methodists in the *Advocate* on January 2, 1963. The statement's creators had arranged with Sam Ashmore to publish in the new year's first issue, and an editor's note announced that the statement came from "some of the younger[,] . . . best trained and most promising ministers" of the Conference and added, "We feel they express the conviction of the vast majority of the clerical members of the conference." An editorial on "Freedom of the Pulpit" ran on the next page.[14]

To many readers, it was bad enough for the *Discipline* of The Methodist Church to condemn segregation, but it was much worse when their ministers publicly suggested the Church in Mississippi should change, especially when secular newspaper editors and many white non-Methodists raised such a ruckus about the statement. The "Closed Society" orthodoxy and commitment to "our Southern way of life" trumped the Church's "expressed witness" for many church members and some pastors. The twenty-eight native Mississippi pastors had betrayed the Southern way of life; tensions between allegiance to the current system and the Christian faith were not apparent to the statement's critics.

Response to Born of Conviction took many forms. The most significant public expressions of support came from Conference Lay Leader J. P. Stafford, a group of twenty-three ministers in North Mississippi's Tupelo District, and Dr. W. B. Selah, pastor of Jackson's Galloway Church. A couple of letters in Mississippi dailies were supportive, and a *Delta Democrat Times'* editorial, "The Veil Is Lifted," said that individual ministers who had "raised their lonely voices of protest" were "no longer so lonely." But most letter writers attacked the twenty-eight, and most editorials attacked

---

publication if word got out. Author's interviews with Rayford Woodrick, March 11, 2004, and William T. Lowry, August 7, 2003; the draft text of a *Life* magazine article by Ron Bailey (not published) refers to a minister who commented, "It sounds innocuous enough," but refused to sign the statement (Dunnam PP); author's interview with Elton Brown, July 10, 2003; and Ned Kellar, "Sandersville."

13. Rod Entrekin, one of the twenty-eight, coined this phrase in "My Journey in Ministry," an August 2004 presentation he made to a church group in Hattiesburg (Rod Entrekin Private Papers).

14. *MMA*, January 2, 1963.

or dismissed them, with one questioning whether Mississippi preachers truly lacked freedom of the pulpit and suggesting that progress might be "better achieved with a return to old fashioned religion distinctly separated from the frills of new-fangled social and complex political theories." The segregationist Mississippi Association of Methodist Ministers and Laymen charged that it "is unchristian to endanger segregation," an institution "which has protected both races and allowed both their fullest development," and asserted that a minister desiring "freedom of the pulpit" should "be ready to accept the consequences if what he says offends the consciences of those to whom he looks for support."[15]

The twenty-eight definitely offended some church members. The Official Board of Oakland Heights Church in Meridian voted down an attempt to dismiss their pastor Ed McRae by a margin of nineteen to thirteen. Some then called for a vote of the church membership, and a member of the anti-McRae faction offered this reason for his opposition:

> We do not believe in integration. We do not believe that all races are brothers as stated in the document signed by the twenty-eight pastors. We believe in the freedom of worship and feel that we do not have this if we are forced to listen to a minister who has shown by his actions that he does not care about our Southern way of life but will betray part of his membership by signing what we believe is a politically inspired document.

The congregational vote was not taken, but in February the same Board formally requested a change in pastors in June and declared "we do not want one of the twenty-seven Ministers that signed this resolution." Several congregations passed similar resolutions. Other congregations were more polite, issuing statements "agreeing to disagree" with their pastors.[16]

Oakland Heights played by Methodist rules and waited until the end of the Conference year for McRae to move, but three of the twenty-eight

15. Jackson *Clarion-Ledger* (hereafter abbreviated *JCL*), January 4, 1963; *JCL*, January 7, 1963; *Delta Democrat Times*, January 6, 1963 (the editor was Pulitzer Prize winner Hodding Carter Jr.); *Jackson Daily News* (hereafter *JDN*), January 4, 1963 (the editor, Jimmy Ward, was Methodist); *JCL*, January 11, 1963.

16. *Meridian Star*, January 11, 1963 (note that Methodist polity does not allow churches to fire their pastors); H. H. Buchanan to Bishop Franklin, February 11, 1963, J. B. Cain Archives of Mississippi Methodism, Millsaps College (hereafter JBCA), Bishop's Office Papers, M63, Box 1, Folder 19; more "polite" resolutions were passed by Wesson (served by signer Rod Entrekin) and Galloway (in response to Furr as a signer and Selah as a vocal supporter)—*JCL*, January 31, 1963, and January 15, 1963.

left their churches almost immediately, two forced out by their congregations with the cooperation of the District Superintendent. Within a week of the statement's publication, at a charge-wide meeting of Neshoba County's Philadelphia Circuit presided over by the Meridian D. S., two of the three churches on the charge voted to dismiss their pastor, James Rush, who was present only because three supportive church members informed him of the meeting at the last minute. Rush remembers someone at the meeting saying, "If the Methodist Church can't get rid of a nigger-lovin' pastor, we know how to do it." By February 1, the Conference had appointed another minister to the charge, and Rush transferred to the Southern California-Arizona Conference on March 1.[17]

At Byram, just south of Jackson, James Nicholson was also relieved of his pastorate in January. Earlier, in October 1962, after soul-searching reflection Nicholson had discerned a clear calling from God to speak the truth about race relations and the Ole Miss riot. In a sermon preached that month titled "Real Issues for These Times," he called for individual and collective repentance for Ole Miss, similar to the statement of the Oxford ministers. Refusing to mince words, Nicholson said, "We have let prejudice shut out the Gospel and in many areas of our lives have turned to the gods of segregation and white supremacy to sustain us." Most of the congregation boycotted worship after that sermon, and when Nicholson went public as one of the twenty-eight, the congregation renewed its call to the District Superintendent, J. W. Leggett Jr., for their pastor to be removed. In Leggett's view, Nicholson's support of Born of Conviction violated an agreement reached after his earlier sermon that "there [would not be] any further agitation regarding the race matter." Nicholson returned in late January to Perkins School of Theology to finish his seminary degree. His family was allowed to remain in the Byram

17. *Neshoba Democrat*, January 10, 1963; author's interview with James and Libby Rush, July 22, 2004. The Mars Hill Church gave Rush a vote of confidence, mainly due to the influence of Andrew Williamson, a farmer with adult children who were Methodist clergy and missionaries (see *NYT*, January 19, 1963). Though the *Neshoba Democrat* article does not mention it, Rush says the D. S. was present at the meeting. A portion of Rush's account of these events is included in Silver, *Mississippi: The Closed Society*, 59–60. Present at the meeting was Lawrence Rainey, who later that year was elected sheriff of Neshoba County and in 1967 was acquitted on federal civil rights charges from the June 1964 murders of civil rights workers James Chaney, Andrew Goodman, and Michael Schwerner. *Journal of the Mississippi Conference* (hereafter abbreviated *JMC*), 1963, pages 113, 100.

parsonage until June, at which time he received another pastoral appointment. He stayed only a couple of months before transferring to the South Iowa Conference in August.[18]

Of all the churches served by the twenty-eight, the situation receiving the most news coverage was Bill Lampton's at Pisgah, just northwest of McComb in Pike County. Negative reaction was immediate, and a church meeting was held Thursday, January 3, presided over by the District Superintendent, Norman Boone, with Lampton properly notified and present. No vote was taken; a few members said they would be at worship Sunday, but others "swore that as long as [Lampton] was the pastor they would refuse to support the church in any way." One person said, "If this is what the churches are teaching, then I won't go to any church at all." The next night, two tires on Lampton's car were slashed, and on Saturday two church members informed him of "rumors of a mob, with possible threats to the church or parsonage" and counseled against his presence at worship on Sunday. "Fearing," Lampton said, "that the eruption of violence might spread like measles," he took his family fifty miles away to his hometown of Columbia and did not return. The Conference paid his salary until May 31, when he transferred to Indiana.[19]

There were varying degrees of ostracism from church members and people in the towns where the twenty-eight and their families lived as well as rejection from some fellow ministers. Most received anonymous phone calls and hate mail. Some received threats either by phone or face

18. Unlike the stories of Rush and Bill Lampton (see below), Nicholson's dismissal was not reported in the Mississippi press in January, though it was mentioned in the *New York Times* story on January 19, 1963. James Nicholson, "My Mississippi Experiences" (unpublished essay from his private papers) and "Real Issues for These Times," *New South*, March 1963; the sermon elaborated on three of the four points eventually included in Born of Conviction and borrowed some language from Ashmore's "Who Is To Blame for the Rioting?" J. W. Leggett Jr. to James Nicholson, January 11, 1963 (Nicholson PP); author's interview with Nicholson, June 12, 2004; the reasons for relieving him of his pastoral duties are spelled out in Leggett's letter and contested a bit by Nicholson in an undated contemporaneous statement (Nicholson PP); for Nicholson's account to James Silver, see James Wesley Silver Papers, Department of Archives and Special Collections, J. D. Williams Library, University of Mississippi, Box 23, Folder 9; *JMC*, 1964, 94.

19. *JCL*, January 9, 1963; Lampton to James Silver, January 30, 1963, Silver Papers, Box 23, Folder 9; *JMC*, 1963, 100. One difference from Rush and Nicholson's cases is that Norman Boone was more supportive of Lampton and likely encouraged him to stay at Pisgah; this is implied in Lampton's letter to Silver and confirmed in statements on Boone from other informants and in Ron Barham's email to author, March 16, 2006, reporting on a conversation with Boone's widow.

to face, and there were isolated incidents of violence to property. At least three (Furr, McRae, and Trigg) had crosses burned in their yards. A few were told by the Bishop or their District Superintendent that "there is no church in the Conference that will accept you as their pastor." Summer Walters, associate pastor at Jefferson Street Church in Natchez, was told publicly at a church meeting by a prominent member that he was no longer welcome in the member's home. Joe Way described his church's response:

> I and the family were ostracized and parishioners came only for Sunday morning worship. . . . None of them associated socially with us. . . . No threats came while there, just isolation. Even though [we] did not discuss the situation in the presence of our children, they knew something had changed. One Sunday after church . . . our three year old daughter began to cry. When asked why . . . she replied, "Nobody loves us anymore."

Although in a number of cases family members paid a high price for their husband's or father's witness, many of them expressed great pride in the stand taken by the twenty-eight.[20]

Each of the twenty-eight also received scores of private expressions of support, both in person and in writing, from Mississippi and beyond; some in-state supporters admitted they were not brave enough to do so publicly. This written encouragement from an elderly church member came to Wilton Carter, pastor at Lake: "I want to commend you on your

20. Jerry Furr response to Waits 1965 questionnaire, Jim L. Waits Papers, Pitts Theology Library Archives, Emory University, Box 1, Folder 14; and author's interviews with Ed and Martina McRae, June 5, 2004, and Jerry and Rose Trigg, June 10, 2004; Joseph C. Way to James Silver, June 17, 1963, Silver Papers, Box 23, Folder 9; author's interview with Summer and Betty Walters, June 13, 2004; and "My Ministerial Experiences in Mississippi 1961-1963," Summer and Betty Walters Papers, JBCA, M79, Box 2, Folder 3; Joseph C. Way to author, April 21, 2004—Gene Davenport and Joe Way were fellow students at Vanderbilt Divinity School in the late 1950s. Some children of the twenty-eight have written unpublished accounts of their family's experiences, including *Born of Conviction*, a play by Kathryn Dickinson, daughter of Buford Dickinson (a reading of which was performed at a New York City community theatre in 2004), and essays by J. Syd Conner, son of James Conner ("The Brandon Winter") and Deborah Holston Selden, daughter of James Holston ("One Family's Response to the Born of Conviction Statement")—all three fathers are deceased. See also the memoir of James S. Conner's life written by two of his sons, David and J. Syd, *Mississippi Conference Journal*, 1989, 395–96. Signer Ned Kellar has written "Sandersville," a lengthy unpublished memoir of his experience.

stand it has been a long time since the truth has been told and I am really proud of you [sic]. We need more preachers of all denominations to pro-claim the truths as written in the Bible." In addition to his public support, Conference Lay Leader J. P. Stafford of Cary wrote these words in a letter to each of the twenty-eight:

> Welcome to the fold of those who are willing to stand up and be counted. There is still plenty of room left for others, and we hope many will join you. For our part we will not feel so lonesome any more.
>
> In the future, there will be an answer for those who ask— Where are the Pastors of the Mississippi Conference? We can say there are at least "7000" (twenty-eight) who have not "bowed the knee to Baal."[21]

The Millsaps College Faculty sent Bishop Franklin a confidential resolution urging him to offer his full support to the twenty-eight (sixteen of whom were Millsaps graduates) and any others who might speak out on controversial issues, "both by means of public statement and private attention to their welfare. We further urge that such men be personally encouraged by you to remain in the churches in Mississippi." The main argument of those faculty members who voted against the resolution was fear that "the public attitude toward Millsaps College" would be harmed as a result.[22]

In the January 16th *Advocate*, concern for the institution of The Methodist Church in Mississippi was expressed in a response to Born of Conviction from Bert Jordan, an Associate Lay Leader of the Conference: "I do not understand why, in the face of magnificent progress, unparal-leled growth in stewardship and unlimited opportunities, that we would bring down upon ourselves an unnecessary social crisis that lashes a stag-gering blow to the church and the unity of our people." That same week the *Advocate* printed the response of Bishop Franklin and the Mississippi Conference Cabinet. Avoiding any direct mention of Born of Conviction,

21. The twenty-eight received national press coverage, both in church press (e.g., "Methodist Ministers Shatter Vacuum," *Christian Century*, February 20, 1963, 229–30) and secular (*NYT*, January 19, 1963); C. D. Parker to Carter, January 8, 1963, Wilton Carter Private Papers; J. P. Stafford to "Dear Brothers," January 3, 1963, Inman Moore Private Papers—the Biblical quote comes from 1 Kings 19:18.

22. Paul D. Hardin, Faculty Secretary, to Bishop Franklin, January 25, 1963, and minutes of the January 24 Faculty Meeting, Millsaps College Archives, Faculty Meeting Minutes, Memos, and Reports, B1, Box 1, Folder 1962–1963.

these Conference leaders said without elaboration, "We each declare anew our support of the doctrines and historic positions of the Methodist Church." They also assured Mississippi Methodists that "integration is not forced upon any part of our Church," and then closed by emphasizing mercy, justice, and high calling, but also institutional concerns: "Our Conference has a great program in evangelism, education, missions and other areas. Let us move on to do the work of the Church, loving mercy, doing justly, and walking humbly with our Lord, pressing toward the mark of the prize of high calling of God in Christ Jesus." Was this the response Sam Ashmore feared when he warned in October 1962 that the Church might lose its life in "pious platitudes" when "courageous witness" was so clearly needed? Did the "Let us move on" mean, in essence, "Let's put this Born of Conviction embarrassment behind us"?

A Choice to Leave, A Mind to Stay

Not only did Bishop Franklin never publicly support the twenty-eight, he also failed to encourage most of them to stay in Mississippi as the Millsaps resolution had requested. By the summer of 1963, eleven of the twenty-eight had transferred to other annual conferences, while two others left their Mississippi churches to return to school and never returned to the Conference, both transferring elsewhere. By May 1964, four others had transferred out, and another left the state for the Air Force chaplaincy. Two others transferred out within a few years and only eight of the twenty-eight remained in ministry in the Mississippi Conference for the duration of their careers.

Many of the brief published mentions of Born of Conviction in books can be characterized as narratives of forced departure: "they spoke out and were forced out." The whole truth is not so simple; the reasons for the exodus of twenty of the twenty-eight, too complex to detail here, certainly included the race issue, but also involved conference politics, episcopal leadership, conflicting understandings of pastoral leadership, ecclesiology, and ethics, and better opportunities for career advancement. Some clearly felt forced to leave because of messages they received from Conference leaders and difficult situations in their churches, but others admit they could have stayed. Ignored in the "spoke out, forced out" narrative is that ten of the twenty-eight were reappointed to the same congregation for another year at the May 1963 Annual Conference session—36 percent of the churches involved were willing for their "offending" pastors to continue for another year.[23]

Many of those who left did well elsewhere, including two seminary presidents (Dunnam and Buford Dickinson), a seminary dean and national leader in theological education (Waits), and some who served prominent church pastorates. Many of them saw Born of Conviction as one of the central turning points of their lives, a defining moment or "touchstone." Several have painful memories of the responses of church members, some fellow ministers, and most Conference leaders in Mississippi to the stand they took in 1963.[24]

The main problem with the "spoke out, forced out" narrative is that it ignores the eight ministers—Elton Brown, James Conner, N. A. Dickson, Rod Entrekin, Denson Napier, Harold Ryker, John Ed Thomas, and Keith Tonkel—who stayed in the Mississippi Conference for the rest of their careers. The widow of a signer who left calls these eight the "real heroes." However, for those who stayed, Born of Conviction has not been so central in their lives, in part because the Conference never formally recognized their witness and more or less swept it under the rug. It became a "dangerous memory" for the Conference—something buried deep in its psyche, seldom acknowledged. At the 2005 reunion of the twenty-eight attended by a dozen signers, John Ed Thomas said that after 1965, "this was put behind me and I went on to other things." Referring to the experience as "like a mosquito nip now," he concluded, "I will always be proud of what I did; I'm not sure whether it was courage or stupidity."[25]

23. See, e.g., Randy J. Sparks, *Religion in Mississippi* (Jackson: University Press of Mississippi, 2001) 237; Jack E. Davis, *Race Against Time: Culture and Separation in Natchez Since 1930* (Baton Rouge: Louisiana State University Press, 2001) 200; and Robert Canzoneri, *"I Do So Politely": A Voice from the South* (Boston: Houghton Mifflin, 1965) 142; I will explore these reasons for departure in depth in the book on Born of Conviction. Note, e.g., that eight of the signers transferred to the Southern California-Arizona Conference, both because of their respect for the Bishop, Gerald Kennedy, and opportunities to start new congregations in areas of population growth; all information concerning Mississippi pastoral appointments and transfers of the twenty-eight comes from *JMC*. Bufkin Oliver was reappointed to his church but transferred out a couple of months later, and four others who left in 1963 could have stayed at their churches (Carter, Furr, Kellar, and Moore). Marvin Moody wanted to work in campus ministry and transferred to Texas for a job there.

24. The "touchstone" image comes from author's interview with Jim Waits, July 21, 2003.

25. Author's interview with Jean Dickinson Minus, August 28, 2004. Others of the twenty-eight who spent significant time in Mississippi ministry after 1963 are Powell

A clue to another aspect of this story comes in Sam Ashmore's reference to the twenty-eight as "some of our best trained and most promising
ministers." Part of the Conference's conflict in 1963 was a political battle
between an old guard firmly entrenched in power (including allegiance
to the past of the M. E. Church, South, its particular paternalistic, segregated culture, and mostly non-seminary-trained ministers) and a group
representing the trend of younger, seminary-trained upstarts who were
committed to different understandings of the church, pastoral leadership,
and Christian ethics.[26]

The three most prominent public supporters of the twenty-eight in
Mississippi, Sam Ashmore, Lay Leader J. P. Stafford, and W. B. Selah (each
born in the 1890s), had roots in the old system but aligned themselves
with the call to a new understanding of church and race relations. All
three paid a price for that choice. In 1965, a year before he retired, the
Methodist Press Association named Ashmore its "Editor of the Year" to
recognize the principled stand that he and his wife had taken in editing the paper for a decade. Yet negative reactions to Ashmore's courage
from many Mississippi Methodists led to subscription woes and serious
financial struggles for the *Advocate* during his last years as its editor.
Stafford had served faithfully and well as Conference Lay Leader since
1948, but because of his support for the twenty-eight and a few forthright
discussions of the race issue in his weekly *Advocate* columns, retaliation
came in two ways at Annual Conference in May 1963. In the elections for
1964 General and Jurisdictional Conference delegates, Stafford, who had
been elected the first lay delegate to the past three quadrennial General
Conferences, was not even elected a Jurisdictional Conference delegate.
There was also an attempt to vote Stafford out as Conference Lay Leader,
but this failed when Bert Jordan, the nominee to replace him, declined

---

Hall (stayed until 1971), Wallace Roberts (served in North Mississippi from 1966 to
1988), and Bufkin Oliver (returned from California to North Mississippi in 1967 and
served churches there until 1982); Joe Way served in Mississippi for six years in the 1980s
and 1990s after retiring from the USAF chaplaincy; Bishop Hope Morgan Ward made
a brief impromptu statement acknowledging the presence of the signers in town for the
2005 reunion and present at the afternoon session of Mississippi Conference on June
6, 2005; "dangerous memories" is a concept explored by Johann Baptist Metz, *Faith in
History and Society* (New York: Seabury, 1980) 88–118; author's notes from 2005 Born of
Conviction reunion gathering, Jackson, Mississippi, June 6, 2005.

26. This analysis is influenced in part by the author's interview with James R.
McCormick, July 6, 2005.

to run. Stafford retired as planned from the Lay Leader's post in 1964. Selah's story has been told elsewhere: he and Jerry Furr resigned from Galloway in June 1963 when the church enforced its white-only policy (in place for two years in spite of Selah's objections) for the first time by turning away five African-American visitors from worship.[27]

"Did I Do What I Should Have Done?"

Near the end of a long conversation on Born of Conviction with Elton Brown, Rod Entrekin, and John Ed Thomas, Brown asked his fellow sign-ers, "What positive benefit do y'all feel like came out of that thing—if any?" Responses included helping to open the door for many major and minor changes in race relations in Mississippi Methodism over the years, encouraging laity and clergy who agreed with the statement but had been afraid to speak, and giving Mississippi Methodists an opportunity to talk more openly about race.[28]

Bishop Kenneth Carder, who presided over the Mississippi Conference from 2000–2004 and made racial reconciliation a focus of his episcopal leadership there, believes that a question many ministers who served in the tumultuous 1960s ask themselves is "Did I do what I should have done?" Whatever else one might say about the complexi-ties and ambiguities of this story, the twenty-eight did the right thing in speaking publicly. Born of Conviction caused a crack in the Closed Society's united front and cast some crucial doubt on the belief that all white Mississippi Christians supported the maintenance of the white su-premacist system.[29]

27. The "Editor of the Year" was awarded only once, expressly to recognize Ashmore, whose courage in the job was known throughout Methodism; see Ashmore Papers, JBCA, M100, Box 1, Folders 1, 3, 6, 7, 8, and 10. Stafford's offending comments came in "Thoughts from a Quiet Corner" in his weekly *Advocate* Lay Activities column; *JMC*, 1963; *JDN*, May 30, 1963; *JCL*, May 30, 1963; author's interview with Emily Stafford Matheny (Stafford's daughter), March 4, 2006. The exclusion of Stafford from the General and Jurisdictional Conference delegations is one example of the Conference's political re-alities—several of the twenty-eight transferred out more because of Conference politics than the race issue. For Selah's story, see W. J. Cunningham, *Agony at Galloway* (Jackson: University Press of Mississippi, 1980) chapter 1, and Charles Marsh, *God's Long Summer* (Princeton, NJ: Princeton University Press, 1997) 128, 132.

28. Author's interview with Brown, Entrekin, and Thomas, July 10, 2003.

29. Author's interview with Carder, November 18, 2005; the four white and black annual conferences in Mississippi merged in the mid-1970s to form two, Mississippi and

Yet such stands have their costs. Antonina Canzoneri, Governor Ross Barnett's missionary cousin, pointed to a psychological and theological truth when she acknowledged that although her letter to the *Mississippi Baptist Record* would wound "some of the dearest people in the world," her family, friends, and church in Mississippi, her allegiance to Jesus meant she must speak anyway. The same was true for the twenty-eight, and much of the negative response came because the principles of justice for which they stood were lost on those who perceived these native Mississippi pastors, products of the church and the Southern way of life, as betraying their "family," the community of Mississippi Conference Methodists—its lay people, congregations, fellow ministers, and leaders. Many of the twenty-eight, in turn, felt rejected by the church, saying in effect, "As children in Mississippi Methodist churches, we were taught of God's love for all human beings. Yet now when we remind you of that simple claim in 'the expressed witness of our Church,' you turn your backs on us."[30]

A few weeks after Born of Conviction was published, Jack Troutman wrote his mother, who was also Ross Barnett's cousin, to explain why he had signed it. The four-page letter is a heartfelt and frank expression of his convictions and includes the following:

> I will not have to stand before the judgment bar of God and answer for anyone's soul but my own. I will have to answer for my own convictions and how I lead others . . . to rid themselves of hatred and malice toward others regardless of race, color, or creed. . . . In all of Christian history, it is not for the Christian to conform to public opinion but to let the love of God transform them into the personality of Jesus Christ who looked upon all peoples as of infinite worth. . . . Who are we to blame for such "radical" beliefs? Jesus Christ, who was the most radical and unpopular preacher that ever lived.[31]

Though there is still much unresolved in this story for the twenty-eight, their families, the churches they served, and Mississippi Methodism, there have been some glimmers of reconciliation. A few years after they

---

North Mississippi; in 1988–1989, the two conferences united to become the Mississippi Conference, including all United Methodists in the state.

30. See the epigraph for this essay.

31. Jack Troutman to "Dear Mother," February 8, 1963, J. Troutman Private Papers (emphasis in original).

left Neshoba County and Mississippi, James and Libby Rush were invited back to the Philadelphia Circuit and attended a worship service in which they were received warmly and with love and apologies by those who were present. About twenty years after Ed and Martina McRae left Meridian, Oakland Heights invited him to preach for a service marking the anniversary of the church's founding. While he was there for the anniversary service, a woman who was a ringleader of his opposition in 1963 told him, "Ed, you were right. I'm sorry." Elton Brown, who had been at Lovely Lane Church in Natchez in 1963, was appointed in 1985 to Jefferson Street, the downtown Natchez congregation that Summer Walters had left because of reaction to Born of Conviction. When Brown arrived in 1985, a few members told him privately, "We remember that you signed that statement, and it's OK."[32]

So let us also remember those who showed such courage as Christian leaders in a difficult time.

Here are the names of the twenty-eight, in the order they appeared as signers of Born of Conviction in the *Advocate* on January 2, 1963:

Jerry Furr	Marvin Moody
Maxie D. Dunnam	Keith Tonkel
Jim L. Waits	John Ed Thomas [Jon in original]
O. Gerald Trigg	Inman Moore, Jr.
James B. Nicholson	Denson Napier
Buford A. Dickinson	Rod Entrekin
James S. Conner	Harold Ryker
J. W. Holston	N. A. Dickson
James P. Rush	Ned Kellar [Keller in original]
Edward W. McRae	Powell Hall
Joseph C. Way	Elton Brown
Wallace E. Roberts	Bufkin Oliver
Summer Walters	Jack Troutman
Bill Lampton	Wilton Carter

---

32. Author's interviews with J. and L. Rush, July 22, 2004; E. and M. McRae, June 5, 2004; and Elton Brown, July 31, 2004.

The Righteous Gentile in Jewish Tradition: A Tribute to Gene Davenport

Margaret J. Meyer

A couple of years ago Congregation B'nai Israel in Jackson, Tennessee, conferred honorary membership on Dr. Gene Davenport, longtime professor (now emeritus) at Lambuth University. Gene has been a friend of the congregation for many years. His regular attendance at services and study groups frequently surpasses less active Jewish members, and his wise counsel and friendship have immeasurably enriched the congregation and the Jewish Community of Jackson.

In Jewish tradition there is a category known as "The Righteous Among the Nations," *hasidei umot ha-olam,* in Hebrew. A person in this category is known as a "Righteous Gentile." The category has a long history in Jewish tradition. In the following pages I will discuss some qualities of Righteous Gentiles, and the kinds of people who historically have received that encomium. In conclusion, I will explain why in the hearts of the Jews of Jackson, Tennessee, Gene Davenport belongs in that category.

The Righteous Gentile in the Bible

Although there are several instances of righteous Gentiles mentioned in the Pentateuch, the example that stands out and is most relevant for our purposes is that of Jethro, the father-in-law of Moses. Jethro is one of the very few biblical personages after whom an entire Torah portion is named,[1] and it is one of the most well-known portions of the Torah, for Exodus 18–20 includes the central tenets of Judaism and Christianity

1. The others are Noah, Sarah, Korach, Balak, Phineas.

known as the Decalogue, the Ten Commandments. Jethro is a Midianite priest with whom Moses dwells in the desert after fleeing the Egyptians (Exod 3:1ff).[2] However, it is only much later, after the exodus from Egypt, that Jethro acts in a manner that gives him status among the Jewish People.

Jethro is steadfast in his own faith, yet sympathetic to the faith of Moses and the Israelites, declaring that the Israelite God is greater than all gods. Yet Jethro is most revered in Jewish tradition, and frequently recalled by modern rabbis, not for his theology per se, but as the wise elder who offered advice to his son-in-law. After watching Moses judging the people, sitting "from morning until evening" (18:13) until he became exhausted, Jethro exclaims: "The thing you are doing is not right; you will surely wear yourself out, and these people as well. For the task is too heavy for you; you cannot do it alone" (18:17–18).[3] He then offers counsel, suggesting that Moses create a hierarchy of judges. Moses is to judge the major cases; "capable men who fear God" will judge the minor disputes.

What is of interest here is that Moses does not ask for the advice, nor does the advice come directly from God; nevertheless, he accepts and immediately implements Jethro's suggestion. Many a sermon has been delivered on the importance of listening to others with more experience, to being open to those from differing backgrounds, to accepting the wisdom of an elder. Jethro personifies the wise elder, the Gentile among Israelites whose advice prevents crisis and smoothes the way for Moses' growth as an effective leader.

In later books of the Hebrew Bible, in the Prophets and Writings, other instances occur where Gentiles offer advice and counsel to the kings and prophets. But the story of Jethro remains the outstanding one, perhaps because of whom it is that he counsels, and also because of his selfless demeanor.

2. He is called Reuel (2:18), Hobab (Numb 10:29–32), Jether (4:11, considered to be a scribal variant), and Jethro. Though biblical scholars have some problems reconciling the various names attributed to Moses' father-in-law, they are, for the most part, in agreement that the names refer to the same person.

3. This version of the Bible used in this essay is *Tanakh: A New Translation of the Holy Scriptures* (Philadelphia: Jewish Publication Society, 1985).

The Righteous Gentile in Rabbinic Literature

In post-biblical literature, Jewish attitudes toward Gentiles were concretized at a time when the Jewish People lived in lands where they were subservient to others. Jews were continually at the mercy of the dominant population. Though there were business and occasionally even social relationships between Jews and Gentiles, Jews were always viewed as outsiders, frequently with suspicion. Writing in such times, the ancient rabbis attempted to reconcile their own fate and faith with the belief system of the majority among whom they dwelled. As a consequence, they developed a conception of Gentiles that acknowledged their different practices and beliefs, yet accepted that everything was in the scheme of God's salvation.

Probably the most important concept regarding Gentiles that Jews developed during Talmudic era (through the fifth century of the common era), was embodied in the Noahide Laws, the seven laws considered by rabbinic tradition to be the moral duties required by the Bible of all humans.[4] While Jews are obligated to observe the entire Torah, non-Jews are considered children of the covenant of Noah, and if an individual accepts its obligations he may be considered a Righteous Gentile. These laws are: the prohibition of idolatry, blasphemy, bloodshed, sexual sins, theft, eating from a living animal, and the injunction to establish a legal system.[5]

The Rabbis derived the Noahide laws from the divine demands placed upon Adam (Gen 2:16) and Noah,[6] and they are considered universal and binding on all humanity. They have their genesis in the Talmud, where we find the following statement in several different places: "The Holy One declares no creature unfit, but receives all. The gates of mercy are open at all times to all and he who wishes to enter may enter." The two Talmudic teachings that follow illustrate this concept:

> Rabbi Meir said: What is the proof that even a Gentile who occupies himself with Torah is like a high priest? Scripture teaches, "with which if a man occupy himself, he shall live by them" (Lev. 18:5). It does not say, "A priest, a Levite, and Israelite," but "A

---

4. Talmud *Sanhedrin* 56–60.

5. *Sanhedrin* 56a.

6. *Genesis Rabbah* 34; *Sanhedrin* 59b.

man." Hence you may infer that even a non-Jew who occupies himself with Torah is like a high priest.

Rabbi Jeremiah used to say: What is the proof that even a Gentile who keeps the Torah is like a high priest? The verse, "Which if a man do, he shall live by them." Scripture also says, "Open ye the gates, that the righteous Gentile. . . may come in (Isa. 26:2)—not that "priests, Levites or Israelites may come in," but that "the righteous Gentile who keeps the faith may come in." Scripture also says, "This is the gate of the Lord; the righteous shall enter it." (Ps. 118:20)—not "priests, Levites., or Israelites shall enter it," but "the righteous shall enter it." Scripture also says, "Rejoice in the Lord, O ye righteous (Ps. 33:1)—not "Rejoice, O ye priests, Levites, and Israelites," but "Rejoice . . . O ye Righteous." Scripture also says, "Do good, O Lord, unto the good" (Ps. 125:4)—not "to priests, Levites and Israelites," but "Do Good O Lord, unto the good." Thus, a Gentile who keeps the Torah is like a high priest.[7]

The Righteous Gentile in Medieval Literature

In medieval times, most Jews looked to the Talmudic and Midrashic literature for guidance. Moses Maimonides, the most prominent legal scholar and philosopher of the Middle Ages, declared the Gentile who keeps the Noahide laws to be "the righteous man of the Gentile nations," with a share in the world-to-come, even though he did not become a Jew. Such a man would be entitled to full material support from the Jewish community and to the highest earthly honors. Although this attitude was not universally accepted among Jews at the time,[8] its influence spread, and it was understood to include both Muslims and Christians. In the Middle Ages, Jewish-Gentile relations became more common, and attitudes of each toward the other changed as Jews became more entwined in commerce and, occasionally, social relationships with Gentiles. The concept of *hasidei umot ha-olam*, the Righteous Among the Nations, was elaborated upon in medieval Jewish literature by other philosophers as well. Isaac Arama (c.1429–1494) wrote in his philosophical treatise,

7. William. G. Braude, ed., *The Book of Legends* (New York: Shocken, 1992) 353–54.

8. For a more complete discussion of the Noahide Laws and how they apply to Gentiles and especially Christians, see *Encyclopedia Judaica* (Jerusalem: Keter, 1970) 12:1189–91.

Akedat Yitzhak, (The Binding of Isaac): "Every true pious Gentile is equal to a 'son of Israel,'" and the concept can also be found in the sixteenth-century legal code, *Shulhan Arukh* (The Set Table), by Joseph Caro. Similarly, the medieval book of Kabbalistic teachings, the *Zohar,* states that all Gentiles who do not hate Israel, and who deal justly with the Jews, qualify as *hasidei umot ha-olam.*[9]

Modern Times

As the Jews entered into the modern era, changing political realities, especially in Europe, affected their relationships with and attitudes toward Gentiles. In France, following the Revolution, Jews were given political emancipation, and in Germany religious toleration of Jews was now more common. In many communities Jews worked and lived alongside Gentiles, no longer isolated in their own neighborhoods or ghettos. Assimilating into the majority civilization became a goal, and adopting the culture and manners of Gentile neighbors became common. Most Jews no longer wished to categorize the Gentiles as different; rather they wanted to be like their neighbors in as many ways as possible.

In the United States, from the beginnings of the young nation, Jews were tolerated and given religious and other rights that were not yet available to them in Europe. Partly as a tribute to the majority culture, and partly because they simply wanted to fit in, the goal among most Jewish immigrants was to resemble their Gentile neighbors in every respect but faith. Similarities, not differences, were emphasized and consequently distinctions between Jews and Gentiles or among Gentiles were minimized. This was clearly the pattern in the early years of the twentieth century in Europe, as well as America—until the Nazi era.

The Shoah and its Aftermath

As Hitler's influence spread across Europe, antisemitism became not only accepted but encouraged and, later, enforced. Jews were required to live apart; they lost their jobs and were denied education. All this created a situation where Jews and the Gentiles of the surrounding culture were increasingly living separate lives. Friendships were destroyed; businesses

9. H. E. Blumenthal, "Hasidei Ummot Ha-Olam," in *Encyclopedia Judaica,* 7:1383.

no longer employed or interacted with Jews. Many Jews tried to leave for friendlier countries; few nations, however, were willing to accept more than a very small number. As the Nazi regime spread and World War II continued, the Jews in those parts of Europe under Nazi domination were deported and murdered. The story of the horrors of the Holocaust has been told and retold. It is one of the darkest moments in human history, a time when people attempted to eradicate a whole group simply because of who they were.

Helpless for the most part, dependent upon others' generosities for food, visas, shelter, even their lives, the Jewish People of Europe found help from far too few Gentiles. Yet, there were those who risked their safety and even their lives to help others. After World War II, stories began to trickle out of individuals, families, even whole communities who, under the most difficult conditions imaginable, risked everything to aid members of the Jewish People. The most famous of these was the Dutch woman Miep Gies who helped hide Otto Frank and his family in a false room in a house in Amsterdam. The diary of Frank's daughter, Anne, has become one of the most widely read diaries in history. Other widely recognized Gentiles included the German factory owner Oskar Schindler and Chiune Sugihara, the Japanese consul in Lithuania who, by issuing unauthorized transit papers saved many Jews, and Pope John the Twenty-Third who, as Monsignor Angelo Roncalli, the papal representative in Istanbul, issued thousands of baptismal and immigration certificates and visas, many of them forged, to Hungarian Jews, thereby saving nearly 100,000 Jewish lives. Even an entire community, the village of Chambon in France, came together to hide and thus save the Jews who lived in their town, as well as those from surrounding areas who came there for refuge after word got out that the people of Chambon would help them. In Denmark, the Danish Resistance Movement, assisted by ordinary citizens, arranged for more than 7,000 Danish Jews to be shipped to safety in neutral Sweden.

After World War II ended, and the new State of Israel was established, Jews in Israel, the United States and throughout the world began to hear of these and other extraordinary Gentile individuals and communities who risked their safety and lives to save Jews. In 1953, the State of Israel officially recognized the term "The Righteous Among the Nations" as a designation for those non-Jews whose valor was to be acknowledged. The Hebrew term, *hasidei umot ha-olam*, was written into the Martyrs' and Heroes' Remembrance Law, which calls for the perpetuation of the names of "the high-minded righteous men and women who risked their lives to save Jews." A commission headed by a Supreme Court Justice is charged with studying all documentation, including evidence by survivors and other eyewitnesses. A person recognized as "A Righteous One" is awarded a medal and a certificate of honor. Originally, a tree was planted to honor the heroic deed of the recipient in the garden at Yad Vashem, the Israel Holocaust Memorial Museum. More recently, due to lack of space in the garden, the recipient's name is inscribed on a wall of honor in the garden. The awards are distributed to rescuers or their next-of-kin during ceremonies either in Israel or the countries of their residence. They will continue as long as petitions for the title are received and documented.[10]

American Jewish–Christian Relations in the Post World War II Era

In the second half of the Twentieth Century, Americans lived among one another with fewer neighborhoods limited by religion, ethnic group or even race than had earlier been the case. This meant that many American Jews have felt even more completely a part of the majority culture, participating in virtually all facets of American life. In the realm of religion, Christians and Jews often joined together for the greater good, working on interfaith projects and committees, both in the local community and on a national scale. Among members of the clergy, interfaith organizations brought together people of various backgrounds in an attempt to work on common ground. At first, close friendships among Jews and Gentiles still remained rare, as residual stereotyping and prejudices kept groups and individuals from understanding and appreciating one another. In the small communities of the South, Jews were still viewed by some as the "other," though among the educated citizenry this became less common. Jews served alongside members of other religious groups in volunteer and professional positions, even entering politics, and in some cases reaching high political office. Yet, especially in small communities, there remained a residual suspicion of those who were different.

10. *Encyclopedia Judaica*, 14:184, s.v. "Righteous of the Nations."

Gene Davenport—A Righteous Gentile to the Jews

Within the context of Jewish-Christian relationships in the United States, especially in the South, some individuals' actions have always stood out. Leaders of interfaith–interracial action on the national level have become well known. But at the local level, one can find persons who have worked quietly and consistently, from a deep commitment to their own values and respect for others. Such a man is Gene Davenport. Quiet, yet strong in his convictions, Gene has always been involved in works that helped relationships between differing groups.[11] While a student at Birmingham Southern University, Gene was active in interracial activities, during years when such activities were considered highly radical. His work there had an influence on actions accepted by many southern Methodist Churches. Later, while at Vanderbilt University's Divinity School, he continued his interest in interfaith and interracial activities. There he began to study Judaic subjects and became close with Jewish faculty and students. He was later to teach Hebrew, Judaism, and Holocaust Studies at Lambuth University. While at Vanderbilt he became a member of the Committee of Southern Churches and volunteered to be an observer during the Civil Rights Marches in Nashville and other southern towns. The objective, according to his own recollection, was to ensure that the marchers were neither harassed by those opposing the march, nor by the police.

After coming to Jackson and Lambuth, Gene became active in the Jackson Council on Human Relations, comprised of ministers who had a common interest in interracial affairs within the community. He was never a marcher; yet, quietly and forcefully he made his voice heard through articles and letters written for the local paper. He would often visit areas of Jackson into which at that time few white persons ventured. He has long been accepted among the African-American community of Jackson, Tennessee, as a friend. Even now, people remember and appreciate Gene's acceptance of all people during those difficult years. It was during this time that he also became familiar with members of the Jewish community. Congregation B'nai Israel and Lambuth University are located just a few streets from each other. While teaching classes on Judaica, Gene found that he had many common interests with the Jewish

---

11. For information for this section I am indebted to S. Joel Newman, past president of Congregation B'nai Israel in Jackson, Tennessee, and a close friend of Gene Davenport.

congregants. Eventually, he became close with members through various interfaith and intergroup activities.

Always eclectic in his liturgical interests, Gene visited the Jewish congregation for worship and frequently brought his students to Sabbath services to help them acquire a better understanding of Judaism. When I began serving the congregation in 1999, Gene was already a fairly regular attendee. Soon he began to participate in our study sessions. His vast biblical and Judaic knowledge and insightful comments added immeasurably to any subject I might be teaching.

When I arrived in Jackson, and for several years after, Gene hosted a radio program devoted to interfaith dialog, as well as his theological and ethical reflections on events affecting the community. He would invite guests from all walks of life, frequently clergy from different religions, who were given the freedom to discuss topics from their own religious point of view. He was generous in inviting me to discuss such subjects as Passover, the Jewish High Holy days and the situation in Israel.

Now in retirement, Gene writes a regular weekly column for the *Jackson Sun*. As with his radio program, he writes on subjects that deal with political and moral topics from his religious point of view, but he is careful to include other religious viewpoints as well.

In 2000, with the endorsement of the board of Lambuth University and Congregation B'nai Israel, Gene and Joel Newman, then President of the Jewish congregation, founded The Lambuth-B'nai Israel Center for Jewish Studies. The Center is a joint effort to:

> [G]ive mutual expression to the common faith of Lambuth University and Congregation B'nai Israel in the God of Abraham, Isaac, Jacob, Sarah, Rebecca, Rachel, Leah and Jesus; to provide mutual encouragement and support for the cultural and spiritual enrichment of both the Lambuth Campus and the Congregation; to promote understanding and reconciliation between Christians and Jews and other religions and cultures; to serve as a resource center in West Tennessee for the study of Judaism and the Holocaust and other Genocides.[12]

Gene served as the first Chairman of the Center's Steering Committee. In this capacity he has been instrumental in observances of *Yom HaShoah*

---

12. From the Mission Statement of the Lambuth-B'nai Israel Center for Jewish Studies.

(Holocaust Remembrance) Days in Jackson. The Center has worked to establish a monthly interfaith discussion group, drawing people from many different Christian churches as well as Jewish and Islamic participants. Under Gene's chairmanship, the Center has organized such exhibitions as: "The Jews of Jackson" and "Living On—Holocaust Survivors in Tennessee." In the fall of 2008, just prior to his planned retirement as Chair, the Center was scheduled to present a three-part symposium on Genocide.

In 2007, Congregation B'nai Israel presented Gene Davenport with an honorary membership in the congregation in recognition of his participation in and support of the Jewish community and congregation. It was the first time such a membership was presented to a non-Jew. Not long after his retirement in the spring of 2008, Gene wrote me the following:

> Along with an office for writing at St. Luke's I was appointed Theologian in Residence. So here I am—an ordained United Methodist minister; basically Calvinist in theology (minus the element of predestination); an honorary member of the synagogue; father, grandfather, and great-grandfather to a horde of Mormons, and theologian in residence at an Episcopal Church!

For the Jews of Jackson, as well as the rest of the Jackson community who have been influenced by Gene's teachings and example, it was a fitting self-definition of a man whose breadth of understanding, decency, and compassion richly qualify him for the designation of Righteous Gentile.

Gene Davenport, Witness

Charles Mayo

No one can write a better commentary about Dr. Gene Davenport than Will Campbell does in the "Foreword" to Gene's *Into the Darkness: Discipleship in the Sermon on the Mount*. Will writes of a boy preacher who attended Birmingham Southern and who challenged the Klan in his small United Methodist Church. Gene was nineteen. No one in the south in 1954 challenged the Klan unless he or she was prepared for the Klan's response, often violent. The boy preacher did. Later Gene challenged the Powers and the Principalities as a professor at Lambuth when he worked with young children with disabilities, children the Powers did not see as worthy to be helped. As Will writes, the boy preacher grew up to write *Into the Darkness*, consistent with Gene's realistic, yet hopeful, analysis for those who call themselves Christian. Will is right: the boy preacher who defied the Klan got older and wiser.

Where to begin? Born in Sylacauga, Alabama, in 1935? Educated (Gene would probably say he educated himself) at Birmingham Southern and Vanderbilt? No. Marriage to Kay? Two daughters, Deborah and Pamela? No. A doting father and grandfather? No. Professor of Religion and Philosophy for more than forty years? No. Professor who brought students to a Hobbit party in a friend's home? No. The person who introduced one of the most popular courses at Lambuth, "The Holocaust," and the man who helped to establish the Lambuth-B'Nai Israel Center for Jewish Studies? No. The man who insisted that he was right regarding an English fragment and that the English professor was wrong? No. Will has it correct when he writes in the "Foreword" that the boy preacher has grown up, but there's a lot more to Gene Davenport than this.

Now some yes's. Is he right about the Powers and Principalities that rule the world? Which rule all of us in and out of church? Yes, as is Ellul.

Is he right about racial and gender divisions that separate us from God? Yes. Is he right that people with learning difficulties and physical difficulties need our help because they are created by God? Yes. Is he right that all Jewish synagogues and Christian churches, United Methodist, Southern Baptist, Roman Catholic, and even Presbyterian have become so much a part of the Powers and Principalities that they, as we, have forgotten the prophetic voice of the Old Testament, the courage and the faith of the early Christians? Unfortunately, but clearly, yes. Still . . . neither the no's that tell facts about the man, nor the yes's that render his prophetic wisdom begin to do justice to this boy preacher grown up.

Gene lives in a dilapidated trailer complex. He borrowed $5,000 to buy the house twenty years ago and filled it with books and technology equipment. The books he knows how to read; the technology is another issue. Thinned gray hair, height about 5'6", with cowboy boots, walks with right shoulder leaning as if he is carrying four commentaries and five volumes, hard back, concerning one chapter of the New Testament, Gene plays the guitar and sings country-western songs. He is an expert on comic books and long ago radio programs that most of us have heard and have forgotten. Gene hasn't. Since he announced his retirement from Lambuth, June 29, 2007, he has mellowed. Prior to his decision to leave the ivory tower, he was obstinate, strong-willed, a bit self-righteous, but consistently clear in his judgments and courageous as well as unwavering in speaking even though what he spoke and wrote were often offensive to those who heard and read. However, throughout his forty-five years at Lambuth College, now Lambuth University, to anyone no matter his or her rank or position, who has done a kind, unrewarded deed, Gene has shown his appreciation and concern. So much for the biographical essay.

Gene thinks that the Bible is a revelation of God, maybe not *the* revelation, but a revelation because God also reveals His presence to Gene in a three-year old boy who cannot feed himself or speak, in the lyrics of a popular song, in a student with religious doubt or a former student with serious personal problems, as well as in the correct translation (Gene's) of a Hebrew text. God, to Gene, is not bound by the Bible but reveals Himself through humans in all sorts of ways, and He often does so in ways which surprise us all, including Gene.

In *Powers and Principalities*, Gene cites the Harry Potter books, *Star Wars* movies, and the re-released *The Exorcist* as examples of our misinterpretation of the Powers as individual rather than corporate. In the more important *Into the Darkness*, Gene uses Camus, Heller's *Catch-22*, the "Declaration of Independence," and Mark Twain to illustrate what being a Christian means and does not mean in the Sermon on the Mount.

Critical of institutional church worship services, Gene thinks many of our hymns are too individualistic. And to show the conservative, traditional part of Gene as well as his familiarity and affinity for the Jewish community, he writes, "we could learn much from the liturgy of the synagogue, which, from start to finish, is a dialogue with God about God's role in Israel's history past and present."[1] Individualistic praise hymns of the contemporary church are to Gene a mockery of God and a blindness to His presence in our world. Gene goes on in *Powers and Principalities* to criticize the praise services and traditional services: they share the same building but "seeing the Body of Christ divided over the very thing that lies at the heart of the church's task—worship of God—the Powers celebrate with glee."[2]

Worse, Gene criticizes an additional verse of Amazing Grace, near blasphemy in the Bible belt south. Do not preach this from the pulpit as Gene would: the last verse "speaks of limitless time to sing God's praise when we finally get there."[3] To Gene, the hymn no longer focuses on the deliverance from the Powers in this world but on the saving of the soul so that the singer can "go to heaven."

Stubborn, argumentative, at times arrogant, why would Gene change? Has the world changed? War? Poverty? Prejudice? Attitudes toward those less fortunate in physical or intellectual abilities? Have those who control our world, those who represent the Powers changed, be they leaders of nations, terrorists, and we who kill the innocent, televangelists who depend upon rapt attention from their stay-at-home viewers, commentators on television who tell us what to think and to believe changed? Technique has; method has. But no change is evident in the continuing presence of evil in our world. Gene will not relent in naming this presence.

Will quotes the old Christian song, "Red and yellow, black or white, they are precious in his sight" and writes that Gene believed these words.

1. *Powers and Principalities*, 48.
2. Ibid., 49.
3. Ibid., 48.

He still does. He did as a boy preacher of nineteen and he does as a man preacher today.

No doubt the works Gene has read influence him. First, of course, is the Bible along with other ancient non-canonical works. Then there are Karl Barth's *The Humanity of God*, all of Will's writings, especially *Brother to a Dragonfly*, William Stringfellow's works, and Stringfellow's visits to Lambuth campus. His debates and discussions with professors and students influenced Gene as he tried to cope with the place of Christians in a strange land, as he tried to cope with his personal life in a land he had never anticipated growing up in Sylacauga. Then there was a month in a Trappist Monastery reading *The City of God*. Geographical distance from his daughters and grandchildren, different religious beliefs between Gene and his children and grandchildren, have never separated him from his love for them and their love for him. Obviously, all of Ellul's work, earlier *The Technological Society* and *The Presence of the Kingdom*, and more recently *The Subversion of Christianity*, have helped Gene in his biblical perspective of understanding our world. The list could go on: comic books, country-western music, church hymns, Calvin, Luther, Wesley. Add science fiction, everyday comics in newspapers, some Faulkner, much O'Connor. More O'Connor than Faulkner, but who is perfect?

Always Gene uses a biblical perspective, concrete. As does Blake, Gene pays attention to minute particulars. As does Blake, Gene thinks the general good is the haven of scoundrels, hypocrites, and flatterers. Here are some particulars.

The student says, "I want to define myself." Gene responds, "Define?" Student, respectful, "Yes sir, find myself." Gene, professional, a bit patient, but rather disgruntled, "Do you want to know how Plato, Aristotle, or Augustine would answer you?" "No Sir." Student, daughter of a Methodist minister, "I don't know them." Gene, more patient, less disgruntled, "Do you want to know what the Bible says about your self?" "No sir." Silence, because both the other fourteen students and the other professor who teaches with Gene in this course are expecting a twenty-to-twenty-five minute mini-lecture. Gene, not disgruntled, "God tells us in His scripture."

Another particular: after *Into the Darkness*, a Methodist minister who had read the book, a good man, asked if Gene "had ever gotten out of the Old Testament"? Perhaps not. Has N. T. Wright? Did Jesus escape from the sayings and writings of the Old Testament? Prophecies? Warnings?

Often philosophers claim we stand upon those who came before us. Will writes in his "Foreword" that Gene cites Isaiah, Micah, Jeremiah. Why not, if one reads the Bible as a written document of the way we should live? Gene tells us that the King James Version of the Bible is not exactly right since he knows the multiple interpretations we all apply to written and spoken language. Never get into a discussion with him about the intentionality of the biblical writers. Since he loves the old radio program *The Shadow*, his conclusion will be "only the shadow knows," or more apt, only Gene knows, not the writer of the old texts nor the person arguing with him. He is patient, considerate, clear, confident.

Another minute particular: a visiting professor from England, part of the UN delegation, pompous and condescending, claims, "As Pierre de Chardin wrote, the UN is helping us arrive at the Omega Point." Gene's response: "I haven't seen it yet, have you?" To say the least, Gene can be a bit caustic when deflating pomposity, even his own.

When Gene reads this biographical essay, he will argue, claim misinterpretation, ask questions, then answer them. After forty years of friendship, who knows? We may see fit to agree on Genesis or Flannery O'Connor or who played The Shadow. Gene or God knows.

www.ingramcontent.com/pod-product-compliance
Lightning Source LLC
Chambersburg PA
CBHW060342100426
42812CB00003B/1094